# ALIVE IN CHRIST

# ALIVE IN CHRIST

## The Dynamic Process of Spiritual Formation

## Maxie Dunnam

ABINGDON PRESS
*Nashville*

ALIVE IN CHRIST: THE DYNAMIC PROCESS
OF SPIRITUAL FORMATION

*Copyright © 1982 by Abingdon*
Second Printing 1982
All rights reserved.

**Library of Congress Cataloging in Publication Data**

DUNNAM, MAXIE D.
    Alive in Christ.
    1. Spiritual life—Methodist author. I. Title.
    BV4501.2.D766        248.4'876        81-20631        AACR2
                    **ISBN 0-687-00993-6**

Scripture quotations unless otherwise noted are from the Revised Standard
Version of the Bible, copyrighted 1946, 1952, 1971, © 1973, by the Division
of Christian Education of the National Council of the Churches of Christ in
the U.S.A., and used by permission.

Quotations noted Phillips are from The New Testament in Modern
English, copyright © J. B. Phillips 1958, 1960, 1972.

Those noted NEB are from The New English Bible. © the Delegates of the
Oxford University Press and the Syndics of the Cambridge University
Press, 1961, 1970. Reprinted by permission.

Quotations noted TEV are from the Bible in Today's English Version.
Copyright © American Bible Society 1966, 1971, 1976.

The Bible text noted NKJB-NT is from The New King James Bible–New
Testament. Copyright © 1979, Thomas Nelson, Inc., Publishers.

Those noted JB are from The Jerusalem Bible, copyright © 1966 by Darton,
Longman & Todd, Ltd. and Doubleday & Company, Inc. Used by
permission of the publisher.

The Moffatt quotation is from The Bible: A New Translation. Copyright
1922, 1924, 1925, 1926, 1935, © 1954 by James Moffatt.

The Barclay quotation is from *The Letters to the Galatians and Ephesians*,
translated, with introductions and interpretations by William Barclay.
Copyright 1954, 1956, 1958 by Westminster Press.

(also see p. 160)

MANUFACTURED BY THE PARTHENON PRESS AT
NASHVILLE, TENNESSEE, UNITED STATES OF AMERICA

Gratefully Dedicated

*To*
*The Staff of The Upper Room*

who have enriched my life,
challenged, tested, and enhanced my ideas
and who serve as living reminders
of the shaping power of
the indwelling
Christ

# Contents

# *Introduction*

The word of the Lord comes to us in a lot of different ways, from varied sources, and in all sorts of circumstances. Bushes are often aflame all around us, but we fail to see. God is persistently speaking, though we allow more clamorous noises to drown out his "still small voice." I am learning slowly to stay alert, to look and listen, for the Lord's reminder that the ground on which I stand is holy and I need to take off my shoes for a while and give attention to what is being communicated.

As I began the actual writing of this book, the word of the Lord came to me not from the Bible, or through a preacher or religious teacher, but from the Pulitzer Prize winning novelist Jean Stafford in an article in the *Saturday Review*. For some reason that has long been lost from my memory, I had clipped the article when it appeared in July, 1974. How it got into my research files for this book I will never know. However, it is a growing conviction of mine that God has more to do with what may appear to be quirks of circumstance than we acknowledge. So there the article was: "Wordman, Spare That Tree!" It was the tag line beneath the title that grabbed my attention: "Hordes of inept writers are grinding out bad fiction at a rate that is fast leveling the forests that supply our paper pulp."

Perhaps it captured me because I was launching this writing project. Though frightened by the word of judgment I anticipated in the article, I read on. The final paragraph had the probing sting of an Old Testament prophet: "It occurs to me with woe and rage that thousands and thousands of trees are being chopped down right now and being made . . . into paper on which will be printed hundreds of worthless and rottenly written books about why we must stop cutting down our trees."

It took days for me to get back to my writing task. I had some of the same feelings I had as a teen-ager during my conversion experience when I was struggling with the decision of whether or not to commit my life to Christ. Though not as pronounced, my mind and emotion became entangled again with similar reservations, and the feelings of inadequacy which I experienced as I wrestled with the call to preach. Who am I to try to write such a book? What presumption—that I can speak significantly and helpfully to what I believe is such a crucial theme.

Jean Stafford had brought me "under conviction," and I could not escape her graphic picture: thousands and thousands of trees being chopped down to make paper on which would be printed hundreds of worthless and rottenly written books about why we must stop cutting down the trees. It was a word of judgment, and I chafed under it. I finally came back to my writing task in fear and trembling, convinced that preaching and writing in the fashion of these pages is always susceptible to that kind of judgment. Sometimes what we do is folly, saved for any helpful or redemptive quality only by the grace of God. And sometimes what we do is the kind of foolishness which has God's grace intrinsic in it—the foolishness about which Paul spoke when he said, "The foolishness of God is wiser than men, and the weakness of God is stronger than men" (I Cor. 25).

That does not mean I always discern what is my human folly transformed by God's grace, and what is God's "foolishness" in which he gives me the opportunity to participate. So, when I speak or write, I do so knowing that I am *under orders* and *under judgment*. I may stutter and stammer, my written words may not bear the passion and fire burning in my soul, still I must declare what I have seen and heard. I do that in fearful consciousness that there is human folly here, but with trembling awareness that there is also the graceful possibility of God speaking through me. I ask you to be open to the Holy Spirit to use my folly and God's "foolishness" as a means of transforming, strengthening, hope-giving grace for you.

I want to express my personal appreciation to Dr. Douglas Steere and Bishop Lance Webb. It was in lectures given in their honor* that I began to give expression to the content of this book. My thanks, also, to those who invited me to give these lectures.

And, thank you, Jean Stafford, for stopping me, and forcing me to get my perspective clear as I begin this writing task. But I remind you, sacrifice is a part of redemption. We may have to chop down some trees to get paper on which to sound our ecological warning against destroying our forests. And I have to run the risk of presumption and even folly in sharing the witness of these pages.

---

*The Douglas Steere Lectures in Christian Philosophy and the Spiritual Life, Bay View Association, Mich., 1982; the Lance Webb Lectures in Spiritual Formation, Lake Bloomington, Ill., 1978.

# 1

## *Rehearsing the Gospel*

$A$lmost every day, for four or five years now, my morning ritual has included a word to myself. Sometimes I speak it aloud, sometimes I simply register it in my awareness. Sometimes I make it a liturgy, repeating it over and over again to a breathing-in-and-out exercise, "[Maxie,] the secret is simply this: Christ *in you!* Yes, Christ *in you* bringing with him the hope of all the glorious things to come."

This is Phillips' translation of Colossians 1:27, addressed to me personally. If there is a growing edge in my life, and I pray God there is, it is at this point: I'm seeking and discovering the experience of the indwelling Christ. I have come to believe that this is the key to Christian experience, certainly the key to authentic Christian piety and spirituality—to be *alive in Christ*.

To rehearse the gospel and lay the biblical/theological foundation for our theme, I want to explore two experiential concepts of Paul—what I believe is the core of his contribution to the Christian gospel—as the root concepts of Christian experience.

In the New Testament, we have basically two kinds of writing. The Gospels are biographical, seeking to capture the life, ministry, and teachings of Jesus. As is the case with all writing, each author of the Gospels reflects a unique perspective, but each still tries to tell the story of Jesus' life and ministry. Acts also falls into this category, telling the story of the first apostles and the history of the church in those years immediately following Jesus' death, resurrection, and ascension. The balance of the New Testament, significantly in the form of letters for the most part, reflects primarily the experience of Christ within the lives of individuals and in the corporate life of the church. Here is recorded the effort to work out the meaning of all Christ was, did, and taught, in the lives of those who had accepted him as Savior and Lord, and were seeking to be his disciples. Also, these writings tell of the emergence of the church as the community of faith with her struggle for the effective ordering of her corporate life, the definition of leadership, and the debate over mission and doctrine. The story is told not as one would recount historical development. Rather it unfolds from the faith experiences of persons—their reflections upon events, their interpersonal confrontations, and especially from the preaching, teaching, and counseling of the apostle Paul through his letters.

Paul is far and away the primary source for this second kind of writing in the New Testament. To him we turn as we rehearse the gospel as the foundation for the theme of this book, *Alive in Christ*. More and more I am convinced with Augustine that Paul is "the person who knew Christ best." Believing that, the potential for my knowing Christ is enhanced. You see, like us, Paul did not know Jesus *in the flesh*. Though he had the first-person witness of those who had been with Jesus, his experience was that of faith as ours must be. He was not an eyewitness to the earthly life and ministry of Jesus. With a note of sadness, he referred to himself as one "untimely born." Yet, he never indicated any doubt, nor would he allow any question to be raised about Jesus appearing to him. More than any other single person, Paul was responsible for the spread of the gospel and the founding of Western Christianity. More than any other single person, he shaped Christian theology.

The two experiential concepts of Paul which I want to explore as a rehearsal of the gospel and the foundation for our theme are *justification by grace through faith* and *the indwelling Christ.* Since their meaning can be plumbed only through experience, I believe it best to talk about them experientially. So first let me share with you two stories which come from our own time.

She was an attractive lady, barely thirty, I would guess. She came into my office smiling, a sparkle in her eyes. This was not the same person with whom I had been counseling. Something had happened. She was changed.

I had not visited with her for two or three months, but I had seen her often prior to that. I remember the first time I met her. She showed up at our church one day; none of us knew her but she asked the secretary if she could see me. I'm glad I was available. I had never seen a more nervous, anxious, uncertain person. She slumped in the chair, glancing at me only occasionally, unconsciously clenching and opening her hands. She spoke haltingly, in jerky phrases, but managed to communicate the fact that she had heard of our church's mission emphasis, particularly our work in Mexico, and she wanted to share in it. If she couldn't participate in a personal way, she'd like to contribute monthly in a financial way. The amount she mentioned seemed astronomical in relation to what I thought she must be earning.

That was the beginning of sporadic, then regular visits together. Always the elements of *doing* something, *trying* harder, *giving* more, were a part of her stance. Her feelings of needing to prove, to earn respect, to do good in order to be good emerged at every turn; very much like Saul before the Damascus Road. She wanted to start a preschool for the economically deprived. She would like to work in a tutoring program in the Mexican-American community. What were we doing about family planning in our Mexico mission? Were we really aware of the plight of the elderly?

As inspiring as her dedication to humanity was, I always felt a bit depressed after being with her. Though we shared a common commitment, and she began to reveal some hidden corners of her inner self, I never felt we made significant personal contact. When our eyes met, it would be only momentarily; she couldn't really look at me. Her slumped body and clenched hands continued to symbolize an uncertain, timid, searching, cowering person.

But this day she was different. She had tried to see me a number of times that week, but she hadn't made it. I knew she had made an application to spend six months as a mission volunteer in Latin America, at her own expense. I thought this was what she wanted to talk about. But I was wrong, and when I saw her, I knew it. She was standing straight. She entered my office with a kind of bounce, sat down in a relaxed position, looked at me smilingly, and began to talk.

Who is this? I thought to myself. Certainly not the timid, struggling, frustrated do-gooder I had known three months ago. It was only moments before she was telling a simple but profound story. All the ingredients of self-effortful salvation had been there:

      . . . trying to do good so God would accept her;
      . . . never feeling "holy enough" or "righteous enough";
      . . . laboring in her humanitarian concerns so she could
      feel comfortable when she prayed;
      . . . straining efforts to make everything right in her life in
      order to sense some worthiness;
the whole scheme of works-righteousness—and all a big dead end! Then she learned that God loved her just as she was. How she learned it is another story, but she learned it—that God loved her and accepted her as she was. She didn't earn that love, nor could she. She couldn't buy it, or ever deserve it. Yet, she was loved and accepted.

Somehow that fact got through to her and changed her

life. She used a marvelous symbol to explain her experience, "I was trying to pry open the window to get in the house when all the time the door was open, and I had only to walk in."

Janet is different now, changed, free, confident, filled with meaning, alive. As Paul would put it, the radiant glory of God, shining in the face of Jesus Christ had shined in her heart (II Cor. 4:6). This is the incredibility of the Christian experience in the life of a person.

Paul calls it "justification by grace through faith" and we will talk more about the concept later.

The second story is another personal one for which I have to set the stage. One of the most, perhaps *the most*, significant persons to enter my life during the past ten years came via the mail. He sent a brief homily in response to The Upper Room's request for sermons on the theme "Under God a New Birth of Freedom." A collection of the best sermons received was to be a part of our "offering" to celebrate America's bicentennial year. His homily was too brief for our purpose, but was so sensitively done, so expressive of distilled wisdom that I wrote him a letter of appreciation. That began a correspondence which has made a profound impression on me. Brother Simon Reynolds is the man and he has become a kind of spiritual guide for me.

I learned soon that Brother Simon was a Trappist monk and was then eighty-two. His letters sparkle with life and are punctuated with humor. Though living in a monastery, Brother Simon is in touch with the world, with truth, with the needs and feelings of persons in an uncanny, somewhat unbelievable way. We exchange letters every couple of months, and though I have spent only one day with him in his monastery in Oregon, I count him among my most precious friends.

We spent much of our time the day we were together talking about *the indwelling Christ* and the *real presence* of Christ in Holy Communion. A few months later I shared in a moving worship experience with Roman Catholics but was

denied the bread and wine in the celebration of Holy
Communion. When, in a letter to Brother Simon, I
expressed my pain at not being given the opportunity of
sharing fully in this sacrament of life and joy, by return mail
I received this reply:

"My dear Brother Maxie:
"I made contact this week with the very soul of you, early
in the week, by mental telepathy and by letter. Wednesday
and Thursday, my supraconscious started registering
'Maxie, Maxie, Maxie' by its spiritual morse dot-and-dash
code. That set me Hail-Marying for the Dunnams and made
me tack Jerry's [my wife] 'Fresh Every Morning' poster
below my daily calendar, to the left of my room door. So, it is
Dunnams my coming in and Dunnams my going out.
"I asked Lady Guadalupe [the patron saint of their
monastery] how to tell Maxie about Jesus in the Blessed
Sacrament. She said use Jerry and the word 'ontological.'
So, He's there ontologically. Body and Blood, Soul and
Divinity, whether I think of him now and then or don't.
Why Jerry? Kim [our oldest daughter] was with her one
month, ontologically before either she, Jerry, or you knew
it—a living existence, independent of your thought of
it—there and how God willed her to be there. As a boy in
church, I remember saying, 'I wish I lived when Jesus did
live.' The answer came immediately, 'You are living with
me now, I am living here with you.' He's been living with
me ever since. Sort of first-month Kim-like. I confess,
occasionally I have tried to dodge His presence. But then my
whole world crashed, and I hurried back to his energizing,
chastened and secure. Therefore, I can feel your pain in not
communing completely. Jesus loved His disciples. How He
hurt when they left Him, when they heard His hard words,
'My Body, My Blood.' The loneliest words ever uttered
were those He addressed to the Apostles putting them 'on
their own.' 'Will you leave me?' I never tire loving Peter for

keeping Him company in that moment of His agony of not being wanted, God though He was, though so hidden a one by free choice.

"I've been reading things about teaching children math. One teacher told her pupil, 'Use your imagination when I ask you, if you have 9 goodies in your right hand and 7 in your left, how many have you?' Pupil, 'Fourteen.' Teacher, 'Wrong, 7 and 9 are 16.' 'I know that,' the pupil answered, 'but you said use your imagination, so I ate one, gave one away, so 14 is the correct answer!' *Is faith using imagination in this sense?*

"Your Maxie image in a mirror has no Maxie substance, but it is Maxie nonetheless."

Brother Simon's point about the *real presence* of Christ in Holy Communion is relevant not just to the Lord's Supper, but to the whole of life. His testimony makes that point. He heard Christ say, "You are living with me spiritually by your faith in my presence. I am living in you by the grace of my love." And his witness was, "He's been living with me ever since—sort of first-month, Kim-like," being a divine coexistent reality. This metaphor of a person coming to life in a mother's womb is a creative suggestion of Paul's concept of the "indwelling Christ," coming alive in a person.

Don't pass quickly over Brother Simon's metaphor of my image in a mirror having no substance, but being Maxie nonetheless. It inspires rich reflection and yields a variety of insights when pondered seriously. His metaphor stimulates and enriches our imagination as we ponder Paul's great claim that the secret that had been hidden throughout the ages had now been revealed. "And the secret is simply this: "Christ *in you!* Yes, Christ *in you* bringing with him the hope of all the glorious things to come" (Col. 1:27 Phillips).

Having looked at these two concepts of Paul—justification by grace through faith and the indwelling Christ—experientially, let's consider them more fully.

Paul's most reasoned presentation of justification by grace through faith is in his Letter to the Romans. That letter is carefully thought out, deliberately and systematically stated, meditatively reasoned. His Letter to the Galatians is more an outpouring of his thoughts from the top of his head and his feelings from the bottom of his heart. It is in this Letter to the Galatians that he gives his most vivid description of his own life in Christ. In Galatians 2:20 he says, "I have been crucified with Christ; it is no longer I who live, but Christ who lives in me; and the life I now live in the flesh I live by faith in the Son of God, who loved me and gave himself for me." This testimony follows Paul's immortal expression of the heart of the gospel in Galatians 2:16: "A man is not justified by works of the law but through faith in Jesus Christ."

When Paul talks about Jesus he is talking about the entire Christ event—all Christ was and did. For him the message was clear. He had experienced it on the Damascus Road, and the meaning of it was deepened as he reflected and prayed in the Arabian desert before he began to preach that message to any who would listen: Jesus Christ, crucified and risen—and all *for us*. The whole New Testament is completely sure of one thing: all that Jesus Christ did in his life and death was, in the words of the creed, "for us men and for our salvation."

Paul couldn't understand how the Galatians could spurn this message. He was boiling with consternation and stormed at them as the third chapter of his letter begins: "O senseless Galatians, who has put the evil eye on you—you before whose very eyes Jesus Christ was placarded upon His Cross?" (Gal. 3:1 Barclay).

Fire was in Paul's heart and in his pen. To capture the burning intensity of this address, Phillips translated it, "O you dear idiots of Galatia . . . who has been casting a spell over you?" The New English Bible has it, "You stupid Galatians! You must have been bewitched." How could you miss it—"you before whose eyes Jesus Christ was openly displayed upon his cross"?

This verse might not have struck me with such power had I read it in another setting. I was using Barclay's *Daily Bible Study of Galatians* for my daily devotional reading during the time when I was visiting the People's Republic of China. In fact, I came to this third chapter the day I first entered the People's Republic.

Placards were everywhere. China is a land of posters. Great crowds gather around the walls where posters are displayed. Posters are the primary means of communication—a method which has been used to share the message of revolution and liberation for thirty years in that vast land.

Not only are posters used for current propaganda, but there are also some omnipresent ones. Pictures of Chairman Mao, Premier Hua, Marx, Lenin, and Stalin were in every school we visited, every factory, and every reception room of every commune. The thinkers, planners, and leaders of the socialist revolution are constantly *portrayed* before the eyes of the people of China.

So this word of Paul as rendered by Barclay grabbed my attention: "You before whose very eyes Jesus Christ was placarded upon His cross." The Greek word which Barclay translates *placarded* in the verse is *prographein*, which was used for putting up a poster. It meant "post a notice" as on a bulletin board in a public square. This is also one of the words Paul used for preaching. Barclay reminds us that in New Testament times the word was used for what a father did to proclaim publicly that he would no longer be responsible for his son's debts.

In the same fashion, but conveying the opposite message, Jesus Christ, placarded on his cross, has been portrayed among the Galatians—and among us. The message posted on the bulletin board of our hearts is *not* that the Father will no longer be responsible for our "debts," but that, through the crucified Christ, he has paid our debts. Faith in what God has done in Christ is what justifies us.

We need to rehearse that "good news" often, because if we do not begin there in our Christian experience we don't really begin. Paul and other New Testament writers used a lot of images to describe this good news of justification by grace through faith. They used phrases like "payment of debt," "release from bondage," "satisfaction for our sins," "reconciliation," the old Adam dying and the new Adam coming to life. Whatever the image, the truth is clear. It is the central message of the New Testament: in the cross, Christ has done something for us which we cannot do for ourselves; through the cross our "lawless deeds are forgiven" and our "sins are carried away."

On June 15, 1979, *The Tennessean* carried on its front page a UPI telephoto from Khoo Lorn, Thailand. It was a graphic portrayal of what was captioned "A Khmer Rouge-style Crucifixion." A Cambodian boy was beaten repeatedly and tied to a crude crossbar. There were no nails in his hands, but his outstretched arms were strung high forcing him to stand on his tiptoes. Beaten and left to stand there in the tropical sun, his death would have been a gruesome one. His crime? Stealing food from a Khmer Rouge soldier. He was delivered from that gruesome death by Thai soldiers.

Occasionally such a current event forces us to see a dramatic picture of the work of Christ in our lives. I have been condemned to die in an electric chair but awaken in faith to discover that not only is my death sentence stayed, a new verdict is issued: *full pardon*. I have lived and relived the doctor's foreboding diagnosis, incurable and terminal malignancy. Then I awaken to a new fact: *fully cured, a whole person*. I have known the nightmare of the desert, the anguishing thirst and hunger that fevers my mind to hallucination; then I awaken in faith to a reviving, renewing oasis.

Paul struggled for an image, as we do, to communicate the full meaning of the cross—the crucified love that frees us and replaces the binding cords of rigid law. And it is all gift—God's grace which is received by faith.

As in a picket line, Paul carried high the placard of Christ crucified that all might see God's love, not his condemnation—his justification, not his judgment. That is the placard of the gospel: we are justified by faith in the dying and rising Christ.

Now that placard of justification by grace through faith, as crucial as it is, is not the whole of the gospel message. Yet, we have allowed this message of justification to overshadow another message of Paul which is just as crucial—his understanding of the Christian experience as that of a person *in Christ*.

For two years now I have been living with the Letters to the Galatians, Ephesians, Philippians, and Colossians. I am working on what will be one of twelve volumes in a Communicator's Commentary on the New Testament published by Word Books (Waco, Texas, 1982). Even before I began this study, my life and study of prayer had convinced me that the experience of the indwelling Christ is the heart and nerve of our Christian pilgrimage. Immersing myself in these four epistles, I have become convinced, with Dr. James Stewart, that this concept is the key which unlocks the secrets of Paul's soul.

"Within the Holy of Holies which stood revealed when the veil was rent in twain from the top to the bottom on the day of Damascus, Paul beheld Christ summoning and welcoming him in infinite love into vital unity with Himself. If one seeks for the most characteristic sentences the apostle ever wrote, they will be found, not where he is refuting the legalists, or vindicating his apostleship, or meditating on eschatological hopes, or giving practical ethical guidance to the Church, but where his intense intimacy with Christ comes to expression. Everything that religion meant for Paul is focused for us in such great words as these: 'I live, yet not I, but Christ liveth in me' [Gal. 2:20]. 'There is, therefore, now no condemnation to them which are in Christ Jesus' [Rom. 8:1]" (*A Man in Christ*).

"If any one is in Christ, he is a new creation" (II Cor. 5:17*a*).

It is interesting that Paul does not tell about his Damascus Road experience in descriptive detail as Luke records that experience in the Acts of the Apostles. He does not recount an outward description of the experience, being struck down by blinding light and hearing the voice of Christ. Rather, he talks about the *meaning* of that experience. Here is a challenge to our witness. Do we concentrate more on the outward circumstances surrounding our experiences with the Lord, rehearsing the details of those and losing the meaning of the events? Paul's most descriptive word about his Damascus Road experience is his exulting song of joy about the deep inner meaning of what had happened: "I have been crucified with Christ; it is no longer I who live, but Christ lives in me; and the life I now live in the flesh I live by faith in the Son of God, who loved me and gave himself for me" (Gal. 2:20).

Here the two great concepts are brought together experientially—justification by grace through faith and Christ indwelling us. My salvation is by faith in the Son of God, who loved me and gave himself for me. It is not I who live, but Christ lives in me.

Return in your mind to Brother Simon's metaphor of my image in a mirror. Ponder that metaphor as you get another scriptural image in mind.

In his beautiful allegory of the vine and the branches, Jesus gives us a picture of who he is in relation to the Father and who we are in relation to him.

"I am the real vine, my Father is the vine-dresser. He removes any of my branches which is not bearing fruit and he prunes every branch that does not bear fruit to increase its yield. Now, you have already been pruned by my words. You must go on growing in me and I will grow in you. For just as the branch cannot bear any fruit unless it shares the life of the vine, so you can produce nothing unless you go on growing in me. I am the vine itself, you are the branches. It is the man who shares my life and whose life I share who proves fruitful. For apart from me you can do nothing at all. The man who does not share my life is like a branch that is broken off and withers away. He becomes just like the dry sticks that men collect and use for firewood. But if you live your life in me, and my words live in your hearts, you can ask for whatever you like and it will come true for you." (John 15:1-7 Phillips)

Extravagant—but reality! Simple, but not simplistic! Jesus came for one purpose and one purpose alone—to bring himself to us and in bringing himself to bring God. Not only does he justify us by providing full *pardon* for our sin, he indwells us to give us the *power* to be and do all those things God requires us to be and do. The message of justification by faith is our evangelistic proclamation which must never be diminished. It is crucial. However, it is not complete.

We talk about becoming Christian in ways like "accepting Christ," "inviting Christ into our lives," "receiving Christ as Savior," "being born again by allowing Christ to be born in us." Whatever the language, the faith and experience is that as we confess and repent of our sins, we are forgiven. We are justified, accepted by God and enter into a new relationship with him. He then lives in us through the power of his Spirit as the indwelling Christ.

How have we missed that crucial dimension of the Christian experience—the indwelling Christ? If we have not missed it, why have we been so dull in proclaiming it? If we have not missed it, why is there so little evidence of the power of this reality in our lives?

Whatever the case, the evidence, or the lack of evidence, convinces me—and I hope you—that the most desperate need of the Christian community is the discovery of this powerful reality, the astounding possibility of Christians being *in Christ*. Not only is the presence of God in Jesus Christ to be experienced occasionally, the indwelling Christ is to become the shaping power of our lives. This is the dynamic of our spiritual formation.

Here are two definitions with which we will be working throughout this book.

*Spiritual formation* is that dynamic process of receiving through faith and appropriating through commitment, discipline, and action, the living Christ into our own life to the end that our life will conform to, and manifest the reality of Christ's presence in the world.

*Prayer,* or I prefer saying, *prayerful living,* is recognizing, cultivating awareness of, and giving expression to the indwelling Christ. By recognizing I mean more than affirming Christ's presence. That is the beginning, of course. Through meditation, reflection, living with scripture, corporate worship, intentional relationship and conversation with others, and other spiritual disciplines, we cultivate our awareness of Christ's presence within us. We sharpen our sensitivity and deepen our yieldedness to his presence. But more. By giving expression to the indwelling Christ I mean actually reflecting his life within us in our daily living; living out of his presence so that his Spirit will be expressed through us. Then that fantastic and thrilling rubric for our lives will become a viable possibility: *we will be Christ to, and/or receive Christ from every person we meet.* With that in mind we will continue our rehearsal of the gospel in the next chapter by talking about dying and rising with Christ.

# 2

## *Dying and Rising with Christ*

I have a friend who is a Benedictine monk. The way we live out our lives is vastly different, but I feel a real kinship, a oneness of spirit with Brother Sam. One of the most meaningful memories, to which I return often in my mind, is an evening he and I spent together alone, sharing our Christian journeys. The vivid highlight of that evening, still alive in my mind, was his sharing with me the occasion of his solemn vows, the service when he made his life commitment to the Benedictine community and the monastic life.

On that occasion he prostrated himself before the altar of the chapel in the very spot where his coffin will be set when he dies. Covered in a funeral pall, the death bell that tolls at the earthly parting of a brother sounded the solemn gongs of death. Then there was silence—the silence of death. The silence of the gathered community was broken by the singing of the Colossian word: "For you have died, and your life is hid with Christ in God" (Col. 3:3). After that powerful word, there was more silence as Brother Sam reflected on his solemn vow. Then the community broke into song with the words of Psalm 118, which is always a part of the Easter liturgy in the Benedictine community: "I

shall not die, but live, and declare the works of the Lord"
(Ps. 118:17 KJV).

After this resurrection proclamation, the deacon shouted
the word from Ephesians: "Awake, O sleeper, and arise
from the dead, and Christ will give you light" (Eph. 5:14).
Then the bells of the Abbey rang loudly and joyfully,
Brother Sam rose, the funeral pall fell off, and the robe of the
Benedictine order was placed on him. He received the kiss
of peace and was welcomed into the community to live a life
"hid in Christ."

This great liturgy of death and resurrection is a symbolic
reenactment of the Christian experience. When I heard it I
relived my baptism in a cold creek in September in rural
Mississippi. Paul gave powerful witness to this experience
over and over again: I have been crucified with Christ; I am
now alive in him.

To be a Christian is to change. It is to become new. It is not
simply a matter of choosing a new life-style, though there is
a new style. It has to do with being a new person. The new
person does not emerge full grown. Conversion, passing
from life to death, may be the miracle of a moment, but the
making of a saint is the task of a lifetime. The dynamic
process of saint-making is to work out in fact what is already
true in principle. In *position*, in our relation to God in Jesus
Christ, we are new persons; that is justification. Now our
*condition*, the actual life that we live, must be brought into
harmony with our new position. That is the process of
sanctification.

A man once said to Dwight L. Moody, "Sir, I am a
self-made man." Moody replied, "You have saved the Lord
from a very great responsibility." It is the Lord who made us
and who remakes us. Two things happened in the fall, and
in our own fall. The first is that we became *estranged* from
God. Second, his image within us was broken, distorted,
defaced. Two things happen in salvation. First, we are
*reconciled* to God; our estrangement is dissolved by the
justifying grace of God in the cross of Jesus. Our status is

changed; we become friends of God. We are no longer strangers separated and at enmity with God; we are accepted by him as though we were without sin. Second, there is the re-creation of the image of God in the life of the believer. This is the reason John Wesley talked about grace impinging upon us and working in three specific ways: prevenient grace, justifying grace, sanctifying grace. Prevenient grace is the grace of God going before us, pulling us, wooing us, tenderizing our hearts, seeking to open our minds and hearts, and eventually giving us faith. Even the faith we exercise for our justification is the result of his grace. Justifying faith is our trustful obedient response to Christ—his life, death, and resurrection—as our only means of salvation. Sanctifying grace is the work of Christ within us, his Spirit restoring the broken image, completing what has begun in justification.

It is this restoration work of God's grace to which we have given too little attention. In my church tradition, the Methodist, we have a glaring illustration of failure. In the latter part of the nineteenth century a revival of emphasis on holiness began to move through the church. As is so often the case, people began to preach a particularized experience as the norm. Doctrines were clearly and rigidly defined and this portended conflict and division. A big segment of the church objected strenuously to particular ideas about holiness, and especially rejected a notion of "second-blessing sanctification." At the risk of oversimplification, the doctrine of "second-blessing sanctification" claimed that in a second experience of grace like that operative in conversion or justification, a person might have his or her carnal nature eradicated so that one could live a sinless life. Unfortunately for some the doctrine was "cast in concrete," rigidly and tenaciously presented as the norm for Christian life.

Just as tragic as that failure was the reaction of the many who, failing to be able to harmonize the proclamation about perfection and holiness with experienced reality, threw the baby out with the bath. Rejecting an altogether too narrow definition of sanctification or holiness, and fleeing from an obvious stance of self-righteousness, they went to the opposite extreme and forgot sanctification altogether. For decades little attention has been given to "holiness" within the mainstream United Methodist denomination. I'm calling for a new look at, and a new commitment to sanctification, the possibility of holiness or wholeness, the restoration of God's image within us.

Paul contended that nothing less than a new creature *perfect in Christ Jesus* (Col. 1:28), "created after the likeness of God in true righteousness and holiness" (Eph. 4:24), renewed according to the image of him who created him (Col. 3:10), is the aim of the Christian life.

Paul uses a striking word to describe our new life in Christ. I referred to this word in the liturgy of Brother Sam. "For you have died, and your life is hid with Christ in God" (Col. 3:3). A number of sentences in chapters 2 and 3 of Colossians combine to add to the powerful impact of this image. You have *died* with Christ and have been *"buried* with him in baptism" (2:12, italics mine). "You were also *raised* with him through faith in the working of God" (2:12, italics mine). "God *made* [you] *alive together with him"* (2:13, italics mine); "you have been raised with Christ" (3:1).

Note the emphatic underscoring of accomplished reality. It is a settled fact that we are dead with Christ. And there is no question about it: we are also risen with him. We have died to all Christ died to; we are raised to all he was raised to. We now have to live out in practice what has already happened in fact.

Malcolm Muggeridge, the prominent British news columnist, editor, and TV commentator who was converted late in life, makes a direct, personal, simple affirmation:

If you should ask me by what authority I talk about the power of Christ to change human nature, I should reply to you simply (and God knows without one word or thought of boasting) *because he has changed me.* I can look anybody in the face today—my friends, my colleagues, and what, perhaps, is most difficult of all, the members of my family—and be sure that they know, as I know, I am really and literally a new creature in Christ Jesus since the day when he came *into* my life.

We see how emphatically Paul states the case when he refers to the future event of resurrection not as the resurrection of the dead, but the resurrection of life in which Christians already participate—which life is hidden with Christ in God: "When Christ who is our life appears, then you also will appear with him in glory" (Col. 3:4). Paul's common phrases "in Christ" and "with Christ" which describe the new person almost merge. The new life *with* Christ which is received by faith and acted out in baptism is demonstrated in conduct as we live *in* Christ.

The Christian is a new person united with Christ. The two overwhelming events through which Jesus passed into the power of an endless life were death and resurrection. Those who are united with him must reproduce in their personal spiritual histories these two events. To be *in* and *with* Christ is to be identified with him in death and resurrection. What does this mean? Again, we must rehearse the gospel, for the core of the gospel is the death and resurrection of Jesus. These two events in Jesus' personal history are riveted together in meaning, though we may talk about them separately.

How we look at the cross—at Christ on the cross—is a huge factor, perhaps the biggest factor in determining how we live. I found a witness to this truth in an unexpected place: an interview with Bella Lewitzky in an airline magazine. Though sixty-four at the time of this writing, Bella is one of the most dynamic forces in modern dance. I was attracted to the article because the dance is a powerful image for me. The interview was packed with all sorts of poignant understandings about life, about discipline and freedom, structure and spontaneity; about the creative process which involves ardent commitment and almost merciless training. The part of the article that provided the greatest insight about this outstanding artist also graphically illustrated the truth that how we look at the cross, at Christ on the cross, is perhaps the biggest factor in determining how we live.

The process of dance creation itself is sometimes not a conscious one for Bella. Her unconscious mind began working on "Pietas," one of her earliest, most political and most story-like pieces, long before her conscious mind was aware of it.

"I was headed abroad to teach in Israel, leaving from New York," she recalled. "I went to the Whitney Museum, and there was an exhibit of three-dimensional, lifesize, statuary figures dressed in real clothing. I came across one of a girl of about twelve, sitting barefoot in a chair with a print dress on. Her hair was sort of tangled over her shoulder. Lying across her lap was a little boy of about six or seven. A black boy. She was a white girl. And her hand was across his chest and blood was coming from him through her hand and spilling across her bare legs into a pool on the floor. 'I remember stopping in front of it and thinking, this art form says "I am to be experienced. And evoke from you, the viewer, a responsibility."'

"I didn't think much more about it. Then I went to Europe and took my first tour of Vatican City and saw for the first time Michelangelo's *Pieta*. It is the shining, glossy, marble statue of the Virgin Mary with the Christ across her lap. Very slick. Very highlighted. Very sophisticated. And I remember my reaction was one of revulsion. And I realized that this one was not meeting today's declamation, being confronted earlier by *my* original *Pieta* at the Whitney.

"Then I went to Florence and saw a later Michelangelo *Pieta*. The same subject matter but so different. Rough-hewn. Not totally finished. And the flesh pulled off the Christ figure. It was involved and it was passionate. So I had these three images. I didn't know then that I was putting together pieces of the dance. And when I got back I began to work on those materials. And that's how *Pietas* began." *(PSA* magazine, March 1980)

Her experience says something about art, about creativity, but for me it says far more. Since reading that article, I have seen the *Pieta* in Florence that Bella was talking about. I had seen the "finished" *Pieta* years ago, but recently saw it again in Rome, then went on to Florence and saw not only the *Pieta* to which Bella referred, but another which Michelangelo did when he was past eighty. Perhaps I had been conditioned by Bella's experience, nevertheless I had some of her same feelings.

My feelings were more pronounced because the *Pieta* in Rome has been placed behind a bulletproof glass as a result of a madman's "attack" on it a few years ago. You cannot get close to it. You can only look at it from a distance, and primarily from one perspective. Not so the *Pietas* in Florence. You can get close, move about them, be with them, touch them if you wish. My feelings verified Bella's—there was passion and involvement.

My reflection on my experience with the three *Pietas* and Bella's article was made more profoundly meaningful because two days after being in Florence, I was in Oberammergau witnessing the Passion Play. Again there was passion and involvement about the cross. I remembered a story from an earlier performance of this once-each-decade event. An American businessman was backstage, following a performance, visiting with Anton Lang, the person who played the role of Christ. Seeing the cross Mr. Lang had carried in the drama, the businessman seized on an opportunity. Handing his camera to his wife, he instructed her to take his picture when he lifted the cross to his shoulder. To his surprise and chagrin, he could hardly budge it from the floor.

"I don't understand," he said to Mr. Lang. "I thought it would be hollow. Why do you carry such a heavy cross?"

Mr. Lang's reply explains why this play draws people from all over the world to that little Bavarian village every decade. "If I did not feel the weight of His cross, I could not play the part."

How we look at the cross—at Christ on the cross—is a huge factor in determining how we live. For Christians it is the crucial factor.

*Being crucified with Christ* was an experiential fact for Paul. We must guard against the temptation that has plagued the church from the beginning—the temptation to take Paul's crucifixion with Christ as symbolic only, or to equate it with the ritual of baptism which seeks to make crucifixion with Christ sacramentally automatic, something done or conferred by the church with intrinsic validity apart from our living a life of being crucified with Christ. To be sure, being buried with Christ is the language of baptism. More important, it is the *fact* of baptism. I saw recently the "death door" at St. Peter's in Rome. Pope John XXIII commissioned Giacomo Manzu to sculpt it. It depicts a series of death scenes: death by falling, death in war, the martyr death of Peter upside down on a cross, and others. Death by water is there, and I reasoned that this was behind the sculptor's theme. We enter the church by death. Baptism, our acted-out-entrance into the church, is by water. So, death by water is a challenging and authentic understanding of baptism. The early church often built its baptism fonts in the shape of tombs to make the meaning graphic.

We need to underscore this meaning of baptism in order to save ourselves from approaching casually that event in a person's life which is so crucial—being buried with Christ in baptism. But even more, we need to recover an understanding of the Christian life as cruciform in shape. "For you have died, and your life is hid with Christ in God" (Col. 3:3). This is no incidental reference for Paul. It is a recurring cadence in his preaching, and it resonates to the call of Jesus, "He who would save his life must lose it."

Two words capture enough of the meaning of the death of Christ to keep us celebrating in gratitude, and continually challenge us to fully appropriate the "benefits." The words are *pardon* and *power*.

We tend to emphasize pardon more than power. There is no question about the need for pardoning grace, and this word of Christ—total and complete forgiveness for past sins—must not be minimized.

This is the point we made in chapter 1 about the cross being the placard of God's love and forgiveness. We will come back to this more than once in the following pages, but for now it is enough to put a flag up at a plot of ground upon which we all stand: the recurring need for pardon and the assurance of God's love. The core meaning of the cross is that God loves us unconditionally and that through his grace/love, we are pardoned, justified—though sinners, accepted as persons without sin. But there is more, and it is the more that is so needful. There is power.

When Paul talked about the death of Christ and our participation in that death, he was thinking not only of forgiveness for past sins, but of a drastic break with sin, a demolishing of sin's dominion and control over our lives.

Again, for Paul, it was a matter of death and resurrection. "Consider yourselves dead to sin and alive to God in Christ Jesus" (Rom. 6:11). No longer are we "enslaved to sin" (Rom. 6:6). Our death to sin is final in the same way that Jesus died "once for all." To get the full impact of Paul's magnificent and vigorous claim read chapter 6 of Romans. Realize what has happened, he is saying, a gulf as wide and deep as death is between what you now are and what you once were.

The person whose life is hid with Christ in God is dead to sin because he is united with Christ's death which has destroyed the power of sin over us. Christ makes us victors over sin. There is something bold and defiant and jubilant about the way Paul spoke of death to sin and the old life by our sharing in the death of Christ. Faith in Christ means "being made conformable unto his death," having our "nature transformed to die as he died" (Phil. 3:10 Moffatt). The fact is that Christ has destroyed the power of sin. Now, sharing in the death of Christ, we *reckon ourselves dead to sin,* and are empowered to become what we potentially are.

It is not difficult to see how persons could get the notion that the sinful aspect of our nature (some refer to this as our carnal nature) could be eradicated or purged. Paul is so bold in his affirmation about our having died with Christ. The perspective we need to keep has also been given us by Paul. After making these bold claims about "reckoning ourselves dead to sin" in Romans 6, he lays bare his own soul in Romans 7, giving us that graphic picture of sin still present in our lives. He says,

I am unspiritual, the purchased slave of sin. I do not even acknowledge my own actions as mine, for what I do is not what I want to do, but what I detest . . . I know that nothing good lodges in me—in my unspiritual nature, I mean—for though the will to do good is there, the deed is not. The good which I want to do, I fail to do; but what I do is the wrong which is against my will. . . . Miserable creature that I am, who is there to rescue me out of this body doomed to death? (Rom. 7:14*b*-24 NEB)

A pathetic picture—if it stopped there! But it doesn't. Who will rescue us? God alone, through Jesus Christ our Lord! Thanks be to God! (Rom. 7:25). Even in the midst of sin's continuous presence and pressure in our life, we can be triumphant. So, sharing in Christ's death is no one-time event; it is ongoing. We claim the power of his death over sin daily in order that sin's power will not prevail in our lives.

That leads naturally to a second truth: not only do we share in the death of Christ, we share in his resurrection. "If we have died with Christ, we believe that we shall also live with him" (Rom. 6:8). The new life into which we enter by conversion is nothing else than the life of Christ himself, Paul insists. He speaks of "the life of Jesus" being "manifested in our bodies" (II Cor. 4:10). The "law of the Spirit" which overcomes "the law of sin and death" brings the life which is in Christ Jesus (Rom. 8:2).

This new life is not different from the "old" life only in degree; it is a new kind, a new quality of life. Paul makes the radical claim that this new life is nothing less than a new creation (II Cor. 5:17). Sharing in Christ's resurrection means being raised to newness of life.

This means at least two things. One, death has no power over us. The risen and exalted Lord conquered death. We do not wait for eternal life; it is ours now. Risen with Christ, the glorious privilege of beginning now the life with Christ which will continue eternally is ours.

Sometimes we tend to discredit thoughts about life after death as mere sentiment. Not so. It is the heart of our faith that God will finish what he has begun, and nothing is finished in this world until God is finished with it. John boldly claims that God will not be finished until he brings into perfect existence "a new heaven and a new earth" (Rev. 21:1). Death has no power over us because in Christ we have begun that new life which transcends death and is being perfected by God.

Sharing Christ's risen life means a second thing: the power which raised Jesus from the dead is also our power. Paul breaks into a kind of singing prayer as he writes to Christians reminding them of their benefits and privileges.

I pray that the God of our Lord Jesus Christ, the all-glorious Father, may give you the spiritual powers of wisdom and vision, by which there comes the knowledge of him. I pray that your inward eyes may be illumined, so that you may know what is the hope to which he calls you, what the wealth and glory of the share he offers you among his people in their heritage, and how vast the resources of his power open to us who trust in him. (Eph. 1:17-19 NEB)

Then Paul opens the floodgates of his language river to communicate the dimensions of this power:

It is *resurrection* power—the power God "exerted in Christ when he raised him from the dead" (v. 20).

It is *ascension* power—God "enthroned him at his right hand in the heavenly realms" (v.20).

It is *dominion* power—"far above all government and authority, all power and dominion, and . . . put everything in subjection beneath his feet" (vv. 21-22).

The working power of God in the past is to be brought

into the present. This is the paramount miracle—that God's immeasurable power in Christ is available now to redeem us from sin, to energize our wills, to heal the sick, to drive out demons, to renew our spirits, to reconcile our relationships.

Is this our vision of reality? Or, have we reduced the faith to an intellectual conception, a set of dogmas, a religious system to which we give assent and which we practice by rote with no impact in power on our daily lives? The power which raised Jesus from the dead is available to us. There are those who are claiming that power, receiving it for the transformation of their lives. Recently I received a letter from a woman who with five others had attended a prayer seminar I was leading. These women were a part of a group of twelve who meet every Thursday at 6:30 A.M. for prayer, study, and sharing. Their fellowship has become the true *koinonia* where Christ lives and his Holy Spirit works. The letter confirmed that fact.

I thought you might be interested in our group of six—obviously thoroughly enjoying the Lord, and each other.

One, an alcoholic, given the simple medicine of love—last drink November, 1973.

One, whose husband left her with two boys—he, living here with a "fancy lady"—she, making it alone by the power of Christ.

One, who has just won a battle over cancer.

One, who has just gone through the anguish of placing her mother in a nursing home due to advanced arteriosclerosis.

One whose husband had an affair—now both ladies are in a prayer group, praying hand in hand each week.

One, who was on the verge of a nervous breakdown before coming to Junaluska (N.C.)—now praising the Lord.

She concluded her letter by asking, "How is that to prove that joy and peace are in the Lord while life grinds on?" Then she added a rather humorous sentence, "Bet you wonder which is which but that's a secret." Those women have made the magnificent discovery that the power which raised Jesus from the dead is available to us who share in his death and resurrection.

Dying and rising with Christ. Does the rehearsal of this heartbeat of the gospel increase and enhance your understanding of my working definition of spiritual formation—that dynamic process of receiving through faith and appropriating through commitment, discipline, and action, the living Christ into our life to the end that our own life will conform to, and manifest the reality of Christ's presence in the world?

We can share Paul's claim, *Christ who is our life,* when by faith we die and are raised with Christ. We may not experience the liturgy of Brother Sam and his Benedictine community, but our lives are *hid with Christ in God.* We are coming alive in Christ. We will pursue more about what this means in the next chapter.

# 3

## *The Indwelling Christ*

Sometimes a biblical passage catches us off guard. We simply aren't ready for it. If we listen, it takes our breath away and leaves us limp. But if we listen longer, give it our attention, the weakness that has come from being taken aback by surprise becomes strength flowing from overwhelming joy at what we are hearing and receiving from the word.

Ephesians 3:14-19 was such a passage for me. Paul is praying for the people to whom he is writing and, I believe, for you and me.

With this in mind, then, I kneel in prayer to the Father, from whom every family in heaven and on earth takes its name, that out of the treasures of his glory he may grant you strength and power through his Spirit in your inner being, that through faith Christ may dwell in your hearts in love. With deep roots and firm foundations, may you be strong to grasp, with all God's people, what is the breadth and length and height and depth of the love of Christ, and to know it, though it is beyond knowledge. So may you attain to fullness of being, the fullness of God himself. (Eph. 3:14-19 NEB)

Do those words leave you somewhat breathless? Speechless? They do me. The climax and the summary is the final sentence: "So may you attain to fullness of being, the fullness of God himself." Bold, mind-boggling, unbelievable, extravagant, radical—with what word would you respond to this heart-stopping possibility? That we "may attain to fullness of being, the fullness of God himself"! Earlier in his epistle Paul talked about the "fullness of God" being fully present in Christ and that fullness permeating the Church which is Christ's body (Eph. 1:10-23). He had hinted at, and now he makes bold the fact that this promise is a possibility for every person: *that we may be filled with all the fullness of God.*

Paul is clear about how we attain this "fullness of being."

God, rich in mercy, . . . brought us to life with Christ even when we were dead in our sins. . . . And in union with Christ Jesus he raised us up . . . so that we might display in the ages to come how immense are the resources of his grace, and how great his kindness to us in Christ Jesus. . . . We are God's handiwork, created in Christ Jesus to devote ourselves to the good deeds for which God has designed us. (Eph. 2:4-10 NEB)

"In Christ," "in union with Christ," "Christ dwelling in our hearts"—these recurring phrases capture Paul's conviction of the good news. Fullness of being, the fullness of God himself, is ours through Christ who indwells us. It is in this reality of the indwelling Christ that my understanding of spiritual formation is rooted. It is in this reality of the indwelling Christ that prayer as a specific act and prayerful living, for me, has taken on fresh, vibrant, and powerful meaning.

It was the passion of Paul's life—and I believe should be the passion of every Christian—*to be formed in Christ*. He stated this passion in a graphic way to the Galatians, using the metaphor of a mother giving birth to a child. "I am in travail with you over again until you take the shape of Christ" (Gal. 4:19 NEB).

Recall Jesus' metaphor of the vine and the branches. "It is the [person] who shares my life and whose life I share who proves fruitful. For apart from me you can do nothing" (John 15:5 Phillips).

In my working understanding of spiritual formation and

prayer, the Incarnation of Christ in time becomes a personal reality in us. Our prayer and our life is in Christ. In a Christmas Day sermon in the fourteenth century, Meister Eckhart put the truth in focus.

We are celebrating the feast of the Eternal Birth which God the Father has borne and never ceases to bear in all Eternity: whilst this Birth also comes to pass in Time and in human nature. . . . But if it takes not place in me, what avails it? Everything lies in this, that it should take place in me.

Spiritual formation is the process of interiorizing the Incarnation. The Word is to be enfleshed in me. Christmas Day is every day. Emmanuel, God with us, is a daily and continuous event.

The goal of Christian prayer and spiritual formation is for each of us to be "filled with all the fullness of God."

The word *union* is used by spiritual teachers to express the ultimate state of spiritual growth, union with God. Christian spirituality recognizes, and many Christian mystics have emphasized that this union does not abolish the separate identities of the Divine and human. This is not the Eastern idea of *oneness*, of the individual becoming nothing, lost in the universal spirit, merged into the flow of the eternal.

I will talk specifically about this later when we come to the dynamic shaping presence of Christ within us. Here is a clarifying word from Rysbroeck who compared the relationship between God and man to an iron in the fire.

That measureless love which is God himself dwells in the pure deeps of our spirit, like a burning brazier of coals. And it throws forth brilliant and fiery sparks which stir and enkindle heart and senses, will and desire, and all the powers of the soul, with a fire of love. . . . As air is penetrated by the brightness and heat of the sun, and iron is penetrated by fire, so that it works through fire the works of fire, since it burns and shines like the fire . . . yet each of these keeps its own nature—the fire does not become iron, and the iron does not become fire. So likewise is God in the being of the soul. . . . The creature never becomes God, nor does God ever become the creature.

As already indicated, life *in* Christ is sharing in the mystery of his cross and resurrection. Prayer and spiritual formation is the deliberate, intentional effort to live our whole life within the context of the life, death, and resurrection of Jesus. So, the rhythm of the Christian is a life poured out and a life renewed.

That pouring out and renewing is the process of spiritual formation; it is the heart of prayer and prayerful living: recognizing, cultivating awareness of, and giving expression to the indwelling Christ.

To better understand the concept, but more importantly, to experience more completely the indwelling Christ, we need to explore further the biblical material referring to the nature of Christ. This biblical material is rich and varied, and I do not claim to provide a comprehensive presentation. Yet, I believe the outline which follows is complete enough to give us a scriptural context in which we can move with a marked degree of freedom, delivered from preoccupation with complex, ponderous, and complicated theological questions which prevent openness.

I am dependent on many, but particularly to Ross Whetstone for outlining the major categories I am using here. If you feel bogged down in the next few pages, please be patient. If you will give disciplined attention to the material, the significance of it will become clear.

## *The Cosmic Christ*

According to the New Testament, Christ is preexistent and co-eternal with the Father. There is much textual support. The Gospel of John 1:1-5; Colossians 1:15-20; Hebrews 1:2, and many other passages, both explicitly and implicitly identify Christ as "in the beginning with God," or "before all things," and as the agent of creation. "All things were made through him," and "in him all things were created, in heaven and on earth," and "in him all things hold together."

The New Testament affirms boldly that Christ is the *agent* of creation; he is the *sustainer* of creation; he is the *goal* of creation. Through him all things were created, and in him all things hold together. He is the Cosmic Christ.

## The Incarnate Christ

"God was in Christ reconciling the world to himself" (II Cor. 5:19 NEB).

The difficult idea of the Eternal revealing himself in the temporal, the Infinite expressing himself in finitude, is absolutely central to the Christian faith. Donald Baillie, in his book *God Was in Christ* (Charles Scribner's Sons, 1948), says, "It is impossible to do justice to the truth of the Incarnation without speaking of it as the coming into history of the eternally preexistent Son of God." First John 4:9 and many other passages reflect the understanding that the Son was sent from God, and was made flesh—man. His humanity was not co-eternal with God but belongs to the order of created things. Here God, pure being, the great "I AM" gives expression to himself in humanly perceivable reality (I John 1:1-4).

The Incarnation is more than a disclosure of God. Through the Incarnation "in his body of flesh by his death" we are reconciled to God (Col. 1:21-23). As we rehearsed in chapter 1, Jesus, as incarnate Christ, lived, taught, and was crucified in a great atoning act for the sin of the world, rose from the dead, appeared to the church and ascended to the heavens.

## The Risen, Glorified Christ, Known to Us in the Holy Spirit

In the great comfort chapter, John 14, Jesus says: "I will not leave you desolate; I will come to you. . . . and he who loves me will be loved by my Father, and I will love him and manifest myself to him. . . . and we will come to him and make our home with him" (vv. 18-23). He then explains in verses 25-31 how he will dwell with them, making it clear that his Spirit, the Spirit of God, will be an abiding presence and the source of life.

Throughout the writings of John and of Paul, the Holy Spirit, the Spirit of God and the Spirit of Christ are indistinguishable and are used interchangeably. In his discourse on the vine and the branches which followed the passage referred to above, Jesus provides the foundation for the later understanding of the Spirit of Christ being with us and we in him. Look at Romans 8:9-11.

You are on the spiritual level, if only God's Spirit dwells within you; and if a man does not possess the Spirit of Christ, he is no Christian. But if Christ is dwelling within you, then although the body is a dead thing because you sinned, yet the spirit is life itself because you have been justified. Moreover, if the Spirit of him who raised Jesus from the dead dwells within you, then the God who raised Christ Jesus from the dead will also give new life to your mortal bodies through his indwelling Spirit. (Rom. 8:9-11 NEB)

It is impossible in this passage to distinguish Christ dwelling within us from the Holy Spirit. We will return to this consideration later.

## The Body of Christ, the Church

In Ephesians 1:23 the church is called "Christ's body, the completion of him who himself completes all things everywhere" (TEV). This is not just a big beautiful idea that happened to slip in somewhere. Colossians 1:18 says, "He is the head of his body, the church; he is the source of the body's life" (TEV). First Corinthians 12:30 refers to our being baptized into the one body by the same Spirit. In baptism we are incorporated into the Body of Christ and made part of the new creation.

In a very real sense a church which is a fellowship of Spirit-filled people perpetuates the Incarnation. A society which is not Spirit-filled in some sense is not a church. This is the church—persons in whom Christ dwells coming together in fellowship, worship, and ministry.

## The Eschatological Christ

The entire thrust of the New Testament sees Christ as the sovereign Lord of the kingdom of God, both as it is manifested in and around us now, and as it will be in the final fulfillment. Jesus himself referred to the kingdom in Luke 17:21 as "within you," and in the same passage speaks of a final day, "the day the Son of man is revealed" (v. 30). Ephesians 1:21 and other passages of Paul designate Christ as the sovereign of this age and the age to come. The Book of Revelation alludes to the final triumph, when Satan shall be defeated and a new heaven and a new earth shall be established. Then in a final act of great power the Lamb will conquer all, "for he is Lord of lords, and King of kings." There will be a final triumph of the Lord in his return. History is not an endless stream of eventualities. We live in an undiminishable hope: "When Christ . . . appears, then you also will appear with him" (Col. 3:4).

The primary purpose of this brief exploration of the teaching of the New Testament on the nature of Christ is to set "the indwelling Christ," which is the emphasis of this book, in a complete context. I want to make it plain that I believe the New Testament message is clear: *God lives in us through the power of his Spirit as the indwelling Christ.*

Albert Outler, distinguished theologian and perceptive observer and interpreter of church history, contends that we are on the verge of a third great awakening. Above all, he says this awakening will be "an unprogrammed outpouring of the Holy Spirit." I personally believe the outpouring has begun and the "charismatic renewal" is witness to this. This current emphasis on the Holy Spirit is confusing to many and in many instances divisive in churches. The reason for the confusion may be that the church has given too little attention to the Holy Spirit. So the response of many in our churches to this emphasis is that of the people when Paul asked, "Did you receive the Holy Spirit when you believed? . . . We have never even heard that there is a Holy Spirit," his hearers responded (Acts 19:2).

Another source of confusion, and certainly the cause of divisiveness, is dogmatism. Too many within what is popularly called "charismatic renewal" or the "Holy Spirit Movement" are too dogmatic, too intent on a system of rigid experience, the ultimate of which is labeled "the baptism of the Holy Spirit." Unfortunately, many insist that you do not have "the baptism" unless certain signs such as speaking in tongues are present.

One thing is clear from the New Testament: there is no awareness of the presence of the Risen Christ to us or in us except through the Holy Spirit, and there can be no convincing validation of the claim that one has the Holy Spirit unless this is accompanied by signs of Jesus' presence, the chief sign of which is love.

You may say it either way. The Holy Spirit is present in us as the indwelling Christ or Christ is present in us as the Holy Spirit. This is the reason Schleiermacher could say, "The fruits of the Spirit are nothing but the virtues of Christ."

Now I am aware that there is difficulty in this kind of talk; in fact some would say it is double-talk. The question is pressed, Are you saying that there is no distinction between the Spirit and the indwelling Christ? Are the two identical? We are in the same trouble here as we are when we talk about the Trinity, God in three persons. The spatial and individualistic categories of our language give us difficulty. If we are tied to rational categories, we will always have that trouble. James Stewart has given a helpful summary response to the question of the identity and distinction of the indwelling Christ and the Spirit.

Certainly it would never have occurred to Paul that this personal Being, this historic Christ, and the Spirit of God were simply to be identified. This is further proved by such phrases as "the Spirit of Him that raised up Jesus from the dead" [Rom. 8:11] and "God, who hath given unto us the earnest of the Spirit" [II Cor. 5:5]; while the very phrase "the Spirit of Christ," which brings the two names so closely together, "implies an effort to distinguish" [E. F. Scott, *The Spirit in the New Testament*]. At the same time, we cannot but recognize that the ideas have been blended in a remarkable degree. Continually, in Paul's mind, they are acting and reacting upon each other. Upon the man who is united with Christ by faith, the Spirit as a divine gift is bestowed; and the Spirit, in turn, works for the strengthening and intensifying of that union. Only in the light of Christ can the Spirit's true nature be understood; and only by the Spirit's aid can a man confess Christ's divinity, and say "Jesus is Lord" [I Cor. 12:3]. By the fact of the Spirit, the fellowship of Jesus was made accessible for all believers. On the other hand, as Dr. Wheeler Robinson has well remarked, by the fact of Christ "the Spirit of God was personalized as never before, whilst the holiness of the Spirit was ethicized as never before." *(A Man in Christ)*

Let us go back now to the image of the last chapter to conclude this one—the image of death and resurrection. There were two kinds of death for Paul as he thought about the Christian life. One was inevitable; Paul might even say involuntary. We are dead in sin; this is the plight of all. Dominated by sin, our life is a living death. Then comes a choice to die. We choose to die to sin, to "the elemental spirits of the universe" (Col. 2:20), and so our "life is hid with Christ in God" (Col. 3:3). This choosing to die is a negative movement; we voluntarily die to our "old" nature, to the flesh which for Paul means not our body, but a domain of power in which unredeemed human nature is in control. That is only a part of the matter. We *come alive* to God in Jesus Christ. We share the resurrection of our Lord.

As we grow in being alive in Christ, every part of our life is connected with Christ. We live *in* Christ (Col. 2:6), and *with* Christ (Col. 2:13). We are instructed by Christ; his word dwells in us (Col. 3:16). Our relationship with Christ shapes our relationship with others. Christ within us forms the atmosphere in which we live. To the degree of our yieldedness to the indwelling Christ we manifest his presence in the world. This is an extravagant and powerful possibility, the meaning of which we will pursue in the following chapters as we consider the shaping power of the indwelling Christ.

# 4

## An Affirming Presence

Thomas Merton, the Trappist monk who probed so much of the meaning of the Christian journey, sought to establish dialogue between monks of the Christian tradition and those of the Buddhist East. In a remarkable encounter with the Dalai Lama, spiritual leader of the Tibetan Buddhists, the Dalai Lama asked Merton this probing question, "What do your vows oblige you to do? Do they simply constitute an agreement to stick around for life in the monastery? Or do they imply a commitment to a life of progress up certain mystical steps?"

After a long hesitation, Merton shared his understanding of his vows, "I believe they [my vows] can be interpreted as a commitment to a total inner transformation of one sort or another, a commitment to become a completely new man. No matter where one attempts to do this, that remains the essential thing."

In that word, Merton described not only the meaning of his monastic vows, but the meaning of all Christian commitment. We become Christian not for the purpose of "sticking around" the church, but to begin a journey—a journey to become new persons in Christ Jesus.

The Ephesian passage (3:14-19) on which we centered in the last chapter holds out the bold possibility that we may

51

"attain to fullness of being, the fullness of God himself."
This "fullness of being" is the ultimate meaning of
salvation, our wholeness.

This climactic promise is a dazzling restatement of the
entire passage. It is Paul's final, lunging effort to express the
extravagant possibility as dramatically as he can. His
preceding petitions give it shape and meaning. ". . . that
out of the treasures of his glory he may grant you strength
and power through his Spirit in your inner being, and
through faith Christ may dwell in your hearts in love" (Eph.
3:16-17 NEB).

Is that not the way we may attain "fullness of being, the
fullness of God himself"—by Christ dwelling in our hearts
in love? Paul repeats his plea for emphasis lest we miss it.
"May you be strong to grasp, with all God's people, what is
the breadth and length and height and depth of the love of
Christ, and to know it, though it is beyond knowledge" (vv.
18-19). I like that! There is a knowing that is beyond
knowledge—an intuitive, experiential awareness that is
beyond logic and reason, transcending "proof" or even the
thought that one needs to prove. The "problem" of God is
not a problem of logic. It is a "problem" of spiritual
awareness and perception. There can be no *proof* of God
other than the personal awareness of the believer. All else is
intimation.

This does not mean that the basis of faith is our own
subjective experience alone. As already affirmed, the
Christian faith is rooted in the life, death, and resurrection
of Jesus, and the consequent outpouring of his Spirit. This is
reality that is received by faith and is cultivated by
commitment, discipline, and action.

We don't *prove* the Incarnation of God in Jesus. His
resurrection and ascension, and our response to him as
Lord, is not a matter of argument or logic. This is, as Paul
says, knowledge that is beyond knowledge.

Our fullness of being, our wholeness, "the fullness of

God himself," is the indwelling Christ forming and reforming our lives until we "take the shape of Christ."

For some this may sound like so much gobbledy gook; certainly it must sound irrational to those outside the Christian faith. Yet, for those who have taken the initial step of faith, who have accepted the fact that God has entered our human experience in Jesus Christ and has done something for us that we cannot do for ourselves—responded in love to our desperate need for forgiveness and acceptance—for those a realm of reality beyond mental or rational understanding or explanation has opened. We *know* it, "though it is beyond knowledge." It is a realm of Spirit.

Even we who *know* in this fashion, however, must continue to use our minds to think clearly, and to keep our perceptions sharpened. There is much contemporary confusion in the words *spirit* and *spiritual*. Paul Tillich made the point when he insisted that the term "spiritual" (with a lower-case "s") must be sharply distinguished from "Spiritual" (with a capital "S"). With a capital, Spiritual refers to activities of the Divine Spirit in us; with lower case, spiritual may refer to the creative nature of our personal and collective life.

This is important to note because there are significant signs that a "new age of the spiritual" may be beginning. In the scientific world there is not the arrogant air of certainty about material reality as was present a few years ago. Physicists are talking about "open-endedness." There is an opening in scientific and technological attitudes. Material and scientific determinism is being yeasted with, and softened by a sense of, and response to mystery.

With the emergence and flowering of the human potential movement, to talk about *spirit* and *spiritual* is very common in settings as secular as cocktail parties and hot tubs. Humanistic psychology has delivered us from our enslavement to a Freudian system that was as rigidly deterministic as any other science. Psychologists like

Abraham Maslow and Carl Rogers would have no problem talking about "being born again." One of psychiatrist Paul Tournier's greatest books is entitled *The Person Reborn* (Harper & Row, 1975); and June Singer titled her book on the practice of Carl Jung's psychology *Boundaries of the Soul* (Doubleday & Co., 1973).

In this kind of setting, when there is an openness to the spiritual dimensions of life, and when the words *spirit* and *spiritual* are not taboo words outside the church, we need to be as precise as possible in our understanding and in our language. For that reason, I feel the need to state briefly, and I hope simply, my understanding of personality and reality. Naturally, I would contend that this is the Christian understanding. When I talk about the shaping power of the indwelling Christ, I do so from a particular understanding of personality and a specific view of reality.

First, *personality.* A person is a being consisting of physical, mental, emotional, and spiritual aspects. All these aspects are interrelated and interdependent. Health or "dis-ease" in one aspect of our being may affect the health of any other part or the whole. As human beings, we are therefore body, mind, heart, and soul or spirit. (By heart I mean the seat of our emotion.) Our fulfillment and wholeness depend on the growth and development of all these aspects. Most theories or models of personality have recognized body, mind, and heart, but not spirit.

As already indicated, the spirit aspect of our being is recognized more and more in scientific and secular arenas today. This may or may not encompass a particular religious or Christian understanding. That is the reason we began this discussion by making a distinction between spirit and Spirit. Denis Duncan has rightfully reminded us that

there are many approaches to wholeness that make 'spirit' with a lower-case 's' very important but do not recognise or give validity to 'Spirit' with a capital 'S.' They therefore recognise (to quote Tillich) 'the dynamic-creative nature of man's personal and collective life' but do not go on to recognise also the essential factor. . . . (of) the crucial component of the 'activities of the Divine Spirit in man.' This leads such people to make statements that are true in themselves, statements to which one can give complete agreement—for example that to be in a loving or caring relationship is to be involved in a 'spiritual' undertaking. That is true, but the Christian stance . . . makes it all-important to go further than this. This integration of the human personality is, in my view, impossible without the 'activity of the Holy Spirit.' This is fundamental to our view of the aims of life and their fulfillment through personality. *(Creative Silence)*

Now a word about *reality*. We referred earlier to a knowing that is beyond knowledge, but a bit more needs to be said. Conditioned by scientific and technological attitudes, we normally think of reality as material—what can be seen, touched, and handled, that of which the senses are aware. Paul sounded the note for a Christian perception of reality when he wrote, "We look not at the things that are seen but to the things that are unseen; for the things that are seen are transient, but the things that are unseen are eternal" (II Cor. 4:18). Our Christian view of reality includes the realm of the Spirit which Paul contrasted to the realm of the flesh. In using the word *flesh* Paul was including more than the body, more than our body needs, passions and lusts. He was describing a realm of reality that is completely "this-worldly," that makes the material more important than the spiritual; an understanding of reality that tears down barns and builds bigger barns for selfish physical satisfaction, and forgets the needs of the soul, that elevates the temporal and diminishes the eternal; that takes anxious thought of tomorrow because focus is not on the kingdom of God. Flesh is not a neutral term describing a "nature" or an "essence." It is an evaluative term describing the transitory, temporary dimensions of our existence, the fact of the weakness, finiteness, and vulnerability of our earthly sojourn.

It is important to see clearly that Paul did not equate flesh and sin. The only passage it appears that he did is in Romans 8:3 where the Incarnation is seen as "God . . . sending his own Son in the likeness of [human] flesh . . ." and "condemned sin in the flesh." "Sinful flesh" appears to characterize flesh itself as sinful, while "condemned sin in the flesh" distinguishes flesh from sin. The latter is true of Paul's understanding. Sin is linked closely to flesh because flesh is the domain of power where sin operates. Sin, not flesh, is condemned. God came in Christ to enter the domain of flesh in order that sin might be conquered once and for all. We will come back to this, but for now it is enough to say that our predicament is not that we are *in the flesh, but that we are in sin; that is, we are living according to a vision of reality which keeps our minds on "the flesh" as the one domain of power, rather than the Spirit. With this understanding, Paul's affirmation makes sense as the call for each of us: "The life I now live in the flesh I live by faith in the Son of God, who loved me and gave himself for me"* (Gal. 2:20).

This is reality for the Christian. Living "by faith in the Son of God" is to live in the realm of the Spirit, not to have the norms and values of our life shaped by the frail, vulnerable, transient nature of flesh, but to be in a new realm, the kingdom of Spirit, where power is ours from the indwelling Christ. We are Jesus people, "strangers in the world" in whom his prayer is being answered: "I in them and thou in me, that they may become perfectly one, so that the world may know that thou has sent me and hast loved them even as thou hast loved me" (John 17:23).

So, reality for the Christian includes a realm of Spirit that is as real as the realm of flesh (material). In fact, Christians have moved from the domain of power which is "fleshly" to a Spirit realm in which Jesus is Lord. Our formation as persons includes spiritual formation which is not based on the limited view of human personality (body, mind, and emotion) but on the view evident in the life of Jesus himself as well as in his words. He came from the spiritual sphere to be incarnate for a time in a human body—in this physical, material world—in order to accomplish his divine mission. That mission was to provide us forgiveness and deliverance from sin, to free us from the bondage of flesh, and empower us to life with him, shaping us into his likeness, restoring us into God's image, enabling us to know "fullness of being, the fullness of God himself."

It is the shaping power of the indwelling Christ that will be the theme of the next few chapters. We begin our consideration at the most fundamental level of all our needs. *The indwelling Christ is an affirming presence.*

Blessed indeed is the person who does not, or has not, felt the desperate need of being affirmed and accepted by others. I've never known such a person. We spend a great deal of our time and energy attempting to win that acceptance. We pretend and put on masks, perform, and seek to prove ourselves worthy. With chameleonlike cunning, we present ourselves as we think others would approve. The time comes, however, when we know the charade must end and we have to take off our masks.

There is a poignant passage in Edward Hannibal's novel, *Chocolate Days, Popsicle Weeks* (New American Library, 1971), which describes the tension in a person who cannot be himself at home. He can't be who he wants to be. Thirty-year-old Fritzie takes the commuter train home.

It was eighty-six degrees and 6:45 at Merrimac station, but Fritzie didn't call Janice for a ride. . . . He walked. Before he was halfway, his crotch and his armpits were soaking. He didn't care. . . . Maybe all this damned depression could go out through his pores and get sucked into his suit, which he could take off when he got home. . . . He could never manage to throw that grim sense of The End that dropped over him every night. Why couldn't getting home be just the second half of his busy, interesting, fast day—instead of the leaden, post-game vacuum it seemed every night? The spirit in him all day—funny, bright, excited—could never seem to make the trip from home. . . . Even when the children weren't aggravating, cruel animals, but Loretta, Joey and Millie . . . and Janice wasn't harassed but chipper with lipstick on and her hair brushed . . . and life seemed as it should be   . . . even on those evenings, he couldn't seem to catch the beat and get in with them. . . . He didn't feel there at all. . . . He was . . . still on the train or back in the city. Some place back there, all the time. Some place else. He kept hoping that one night *he* would catch up with *him* and it would be Fritzie himself who walked in that door.

The fact that it is *at home* where Fritzie feels not himself makes it even more tragic. Robert Frost wrote, "Home is the place where, when you have to go there,/They have to take you in." Home is "Something you somehow haven't to deserve." Fritzie didn't know that, didn't feel it. And the world is full of Fritzies who cannot be themselves. Most of them cannot be themselves because they don't feel they are a self worth being!

The sixties and seventies were a time when we realized our desperate need to deal with the self. The full-blooming of humanistic psychology, with a focus on self-actualization and self-affirmation became a source of great hope and health for many, myself included. The "human potential movement" encompassed myriad expressions of response to this ravaging need deep within our lives—the need for love and affirmation, the need to feel accepted and worthy.

It is an indictment against the church that secular movements during the past two decades have addressed this desperate need of persons with more imagination, intentionality and directness than the church.

Each of us is someone special. However that revelation comes, it must come if we are to be whole. Though we are all human, each of us is unique. No one else is exactly like you; no one else is like me. *Average* and *normal* are abstract categories used to describe people, true only in general, never in particular. In his book *The Person in the Womb* (Dodd, Mead, 1968) Dr. N. J. Berrill put it:

Every person needs to know, and to know as a child, that he is the only one of his kind and that his companions are each different in ways of their own and demand respect for what they are. He needs to know that whether his gifts are large or small they are his own, and that he sees the world around him in a somewhat different way than has ever been seen before.

Every person is a miracle of existence.

Do we accept it because a doctor tells us it is so—that we are *a miracle of existence*? Jesus said so two thousand years before Dr. Berrill. "Are not five sparrows sold for two pennies? And not one of them is forgotten before God. Why, even the hairs on your head are all numbered. Fear not; you are of more value than many sparrows" (Luke 12:6-7). The marvelously liberating message of Christianity is that you are important in yourself. Unlike much of the current psychological emphasis, the Christian faith affirms the fact that we gain our importance in relationship to God and not in relationship to other people. It is that relationship to God in which we are declared to be precious and ultimately important that can make our affirmation complete. This is not to discount the importance of interpersonal affirming relationships. It is to say that the spirit aspect of our being requires Spirit affirmation.

The Upper Room has launched in the United States and is providing leadership for a movement called *Emmaus*. At the heart of this movement is a seventy-two-hour experience of persons living together in community, hearing numerous talks all centered on the grace of God, seeking to appropriate the meaning of that core message of Christianity by dialoguing in small table groups, praying and worshiping together, celebrating Holy Communion, and spending time in silence reflecting on the meaning of God's grace in our personal lives. This seventy-two-hour "Walk to Emmaus" closes with the participants having the opportunity to share what they have personally experienced during the seventy-two hours, and how they intend to incorporate their experience into the whole of their lives.

By far the most common experience shared is that of becoming overwhelmingly aware of God's love and acceptance. It is common in that it is witnessed to over and over again, yet it is unique because it comes out of the *miracle of existence* of each person. I was moved to tears of sadness and joy recently as a young woman, six months pregnant with her second child, through stifled sobs shared her experience. She had come to Emmaus an emotional wreck. Had I not known some of her same feelings, and had I not spent countless hours counseling with people in the same ravaging destructive dilemma, I would have found it extremely difficult to believe her confession. She was a beautiful person, alive in personality, attractive in every way, having all those things the world counts important going for her. Yet she said something like this: "I have felt ugly inside, unworthy, undeserving of the love of my husband and my little boy. I've had horrible thoughts about how I'm going to love this little one soon to be born because I feel so unlovable and incapable of love myself."

She smiled broadly through her tears, her face was radiant and her eyes danced with joy as she said that during the weekend she had, for the first time in her life, accepted the fact that God loved her unconditionally—that the presence of Christ in the community had become real in her own life, affirming her, and she could go home to accept the love of her husband and son, and wait with joyous anticipation the birth of her new child, knowing that she would be worthy of that child's love, and could love the child without reservation.

That woman's confession is made over and over again in different ways and in varying intensity. The unfortunate thing is that to experience the love and acceptance of God on one occasion is not enough.

What is the key then? *Self-affirmation comes when we accept the fact that God knows us thoroughly and loves us thoroughly. Knowing that we are pardoned, accepted, and affirmed by God is the dynamic that makes possible our acceptance of ourselves.*

This love and acceptance of God is kept alive in our lives by the indwelling Christ. Paul wrote those "new"

Christians in Colossae, "Just as you received Christ Jesus the Lord, so go on living in him—in simple faith. Yes, be rooted in him and founded upon him, continually strengthened by the faith as you were taught it and your lives will overflow with joy and thankfulness" (Col. 2:6-7 Phillips).

Our Christian faith journey begins with our acceptance of the incredible fact of our unconditional acceptance by God. Nothing we can do can earn or prove our worth. Our value in God's sight has been affirmed once and for all by the gift of Jesus Christ in death on our behalf. We continue on our Christian journey, as forgiven and affirmed people, as we allow our lives to be shaped by the indwelling Christ who keeps affirming us in our worth and impelling us to "fullness of being, the fullness of God himself."

# 5

## *A Forgiving and Healing Presence*

In my present ministry I travel the nation, and to some degree the world, preaching, teaching, leading retreats and seminars. While I was the pastor of a local church, I had the opportunity of being *with* people in depth over long periods of time. Now, in this special ministry, I have to make the most of twenty-four or forty-eight hours, or at the most three or four days. I believe the Spirit facilitates deep, honest, and redemptive sharing between persons who, without an openness to the Spirit, would be strangers, sharing only superficially. When we genuinely care for others and are available in love to them, the Spirit creates a spontaneous openness that enables people to be vulnerable and share at deep levels. In relationships grounded in the Spirit, there is a kind of transparency that is unnatural under ordinary circumstances. Such quality of relationship causes "deep to call unto deep." So even though I am with people for short periods of time, I often experience a "meeting" of such depth and quality that there is no explanation other than the presence of the indwelling Christ in the encounter.

Much of my present ministry is also connected with my writing. Because I seek to write out of my own experience, sharing who I am—my weakness and failure, my struggle and pain, as well as my strength, and health, and joy—people seem quite willing to share their lives with me, openly and honestly.

I relate this personal reflection because as a result of these two facets of my ministry (short-term encounters and my books) I receive and write a lot of letters. This becomes another facet of my ministry. Recently I received a letter from a woman I did not know. I was moved by the fact that she trusted me because of my position.

Dear Mr. Dunnam: I wish to ask you a confidential question. For I believe you [are] a good man being a World Editor of such a good book "The Upper Room." I *love* it. My husband was in his seventies, I was a little younger. I never had refused him until now—I always when he wished let him do as young married people did all through life. I had 5 children, 4 boys, 1 girl. I lost my daughter. I have 4 fine boys I am proud of. We go through lots and feel different—I refused my husband—I don't know why I did. His health wasn't good and he died suddenly. Before I ask his pardon. My reason mainly for asking you is because I feel guilty about it. If I could go over that I would do *everything* regardless. I am sorry for all I have done wrong. I have ask my Dear Lord to forgive me numbers of times. Tell me what to do. Just try to forget the past? Be good to everybody? Believe and trust my Lord? I have been converted and am trying to do everything right. I want your help. Pray for me.

It takes more than a casual reading to get the impact of this confession. I have an idea modesty prevented the woman from saying more specifically that she had refused an occasion to have sexual intercourse with her husband. Most of us would not even think there was anything critical at stake in what she was feeling. But don't get tangled up in your own thoughts about women of an older generation being too subservient, or the mind-set that women were always to be sexually submissive. That misses the point altogether. This woman was experiencing a ravaging guilt. One doesn't write a stranger about such a "failure" unless something very deep and painful is going on.

I could share other letters, or recall countless experiences to illustrate the need for forgiveness. I tell of this one because of the uniqueness of it: a woman in her seventies is plagued by guilt because she once refused sexual intercourse with her husband. That dramatically makes the point that guilt, whether we think it legitimate or not, is one of our most devastating problems. Guilt is a positive force in our lives when it is a sign of our sensitivity to sin, or an awareness of a failure in a relationship. Yet, it can be a paralyzing force as well. Whether legitimate or illegitimate, guilt is a burden that will weigh us down, bury us in remorse and self-condemnation, and thus make us impotent.

I sat for two hours recently with one of my dearest friends. She and her husband were members of the congregation I organized my first year out of seminary. Our relationship has been a lively one through these twenty-plus years. My wife and I always felt theirs was a model marriage. Love abounded. Within the family the expression of affection was spontaneous and free. They had three boys, again models of happiness, growth, and togetherness.

I had not seen my friend for a year. I knew from our correspondence that a recent family event was devastating. One of her sons was going through his second divorce, and he was less than thirty years old. Another son had divorced five years previously. My friend—I think illegitimately but nevertheless genuinely—is overwhelmed with guilt. Her big question, What did we do or fail to do in relation to our boys? Three divorces in a family is a pretty heavy load.

I tried to convince her of the power of Christ to lift that burden of guilt. Even if she did have some responsibility in the matter, God forgives. *The indwelling Christ is a forgiving presence,* making us aware of a double need in our lives—the need to be forgiven, and the need to forgive others. As a living presence in our lives, Christ continues the ministry he not only preached but practiced during his earthly life.

By his very presence, as well as in his teaching, Jesus

heightened people's awareness of sin in their lives. Recall
the "fish story" in Luke 5. Jesus had sought some time alone
early one morning. The day before, he had been constantly
involved, teaching and healing. Even into the night "all
who had friends suffering from one disease or another
brought them to him; and he laid his hands on them one by
one and cured them" (Luke 4:40 NEB). So the next morning
Jesus made his way to a lonely spot by the sea; but the
people found him, crowded in upon him to hear and
experience the good news. Weary fishermen came in from a
discouraging night of toiling without catching anything.
Jesus asked one of them, Simon, to take him out into the sea
a bit from the land, that he might speak to the people on the
shore. Here is a telling sign of Jesus' sensitivity to people's
unique situation and specific needs. He knew what Simon
was experiencing—frustration over no fish, a long night of
weary labor, questioning curiosity about what Jesus was
teaching, doubts about why the crowd would be pressing in
to hear this "strange man," a deep need for a sign to confirm
Jesus' right to the claims he was making. So Jesus, when he
had finished his teaching, without any explanation, told
Simon to move out into deeper waters and cast his nets for a
great catch. Strange it was that Simon made no strong
protest; he only set it down for the record that they had
fished all night without any result. He did what Jesus said,
and his nets almost burst open as he pulled in the massive
catch.

Then came the epiphany. In the presence of Jesus, Simon
saw himself clearly: "Depart from me, for I am a sinful man,
O Lord" (Luke 5:8). That's the way it was. In Jesus' presence
people saw themselves as they were. When they heard his
words they also had to reckon with the sin in their lives,
their stunted spiritual growth, their broken relationships,
their ego-centered preoccupation with self.

Forgiveness was at the heart of Jesus' teaching and
ministry, because he knew that forgiveness was a restorative, healing event. Then, as now, many had to have their

consciousness raised about the fact of sin in their lives—the disordered relationships that result, the close connection between sin and disease; the fact that wholeness is dependent on a restoration of our relationship with God, which restoration unclogs the spring of love and forgiveness so that it may flow from us to heal our broken relationships with others.

Maybe we can see this best by looking at specific accounts in the Gospels of Jesus' dealing with sinners.

### *The Call of Simon Peter (Luke 5:1-11)*

We have already recounted this story. It is one of the most trenchant examples of a person having the courage to face himself as he was. Simon's is a sharp confession, so tellingly candid and unembellished with excuses and rationalization that we are forced to ponder long and deep the power of Jesus to evoke such a startling straightforward confession. No enumeration of sins, just an unforgettable sentence that reveals Simon's soul as he perceived himself in the presence of Jesus: "Depart from me [Lord], for I am a sinful man."

Like a diamond, this story shines because of its different facets. It is in a setting of concern and love. Jesus did not hold Simon in contempt, did not condemn him. Obviously, Jesus was a loving, non-threatening presence for Simon. Whatever fears he has are allayed by Jesus' word, "Do not be afraid." Then there is the call to Simon and the others—a call that comes in the context of recognized need and acknowledged sin. "Henceforth you will be catching men." When they got back to the shore, they left everything, and followed Jesus.

### *The Sinner in the House of Simon (Luke 7:36-50)*

There is irony in this story. The power of redemption and restoration is dramatically set forth as the focus of judgment moves from the disreputable woman to the upright citizen

whose party she had "crashed." Rehearse the story. Jesus
has been invited to dinner with Simon. What started out to
be a very *proper* evening of good food and conversation
turned into a shocking display of unabashed love and
gratitude on the part of a "woman of the streets," a response
of tender compassion and forgiveness to her from Jesus,
and a stern condemnation by Jesus of Simon for his lack of
love and compassion.

The woman comes to the party uninvited. She washed
Jesus' feet with tears of repentance, dried them with her
hair, and anointed them with the ointment she had
brought. Simon said to himself, "If this man were a
prophet, he would have known who and what sort of
woman this is who is touching him, for she is a sinner" (v.
39). Jesus knew what Simon was thinking. Had Simon been
so shocked by what was happening that what he was saying
to himself he was actually saying aloud?

This is where Jesus changes the focus. He tells a story that
forces Simon to see not only himself in clear light but also
the woman. The one who is forgiven most loves most. But
the biggest revelation comes when Jesus turns the spotlight
back to the woman and announces unequivocably: "Therefore I tell you, her sins, which are many, are forgiven, for
she loved much; but he who is forgiven little, loves little" (v.
47). Then to make it direct and personal; he turns to the
woman and says, "Your sins are forgiven" (v. 48).

Don't miss what happens here. Unlike all the rest at the
dinner, *Jesus separates sin and sinner.* Before the dinner Jesus
had been accused of being a glutton and a drunkard, of
being a friend of tax collectors and sinners. The idea was
that we should not have any relationship with those "unlike
our kind." So Jesus puts to death the notion that we are to
remove ourselves from the world, that holiness requires
separation. We need not fear contamination, he is saying.
As this woman ministered to Jesus, so others, no matter
who or what they are, may minister to us. Jesus restored the
self-worth and self-esteem of that woman by forgiveness,

by unshackling and unburdening her from the reputation that no one seemed willing to forgive and/or to forget.

## *The Woman Caught in Adultery (John 8:1-11)*

In the previous story the woman's reputation condemns her. Here the woman is actually caught in the act of adultery. Jesus is caught in a "no win" dilemma. If he elects to show mercy on the woman and free her, he will clearly be disobeying Jewish law; if he condemns her—or does not intervene in preventing condemnation—he will be going against everything he has taught about compassion and forgiveness.

The problem is clear—sin and the need of forgiveness. Yet again Jesus does not deal alone with the sin of the woman. In fact he focuses first, not on the woman's sin, but on that of her accusers. They must have been shocked speechless, immobilized by Jesus' offer, "Let him who is without sin among you be the first to throw a stone at her" (John 8:7). Jesus then bends over to write in the sand. Was he allowing the people some relief from their engagement with him in order that they might deal with their own consciences? Or, did he write something that probed even more deeply and burned more searingly upon their calloused hearts? Whatever, when he arose there was no one present to condemn the woman, and Jesus announced to her his forgiveness and his call to a new life.

In her book *Learning to Forgive* Doris Donnelly offers a perceptive and challenging commentary on this action of Jesus. She says that he bound "the accusers to their sins to render them capable of repentance. On the other hand, He offers to free the accused woman from the weight of her shame and guilt by forgiving her sin."

## *The Story of Zacchaeus (Luke 19:1-10)*

Zacchaeus is introduced as a "sinner." Those who designated him so may not have connected the label with the real problem of Zacchaeus. He obviously was separated from God and separated from his neighbors by the place he had given to his material wealth in the ordering of his life. He knew he was "lost," and he knew that he had to do something about it. "Half of my goods I give to the poor; and if I have defrauded any one of anything, I restore it fourfold" (Luke 19:8).

This expression of need and a willingness to make restitution is followed by an illuminating comment of Jesus: "Today salvation has come to this house. . . . For the Son of man came to seek and to save the lost" (vv. 9-10). The ministry of Jesus is *salvation*, restoration to wholeness, bringing the "lost"—those who are not where they should be in relation to God, those who are "out of place"—back home. Forgiveness is the dynamic of restoration. The prodigal son was forgiven, taken back into the family circle, and the father exclaims that "my son was dead, and is alive again; he was lost, and is found" (Luke 15:24).

There are other stories of Jesus freely extending forgiveness to people caught in the ravages of sin and guilt. These stories are enough to make the case that forgiveness was at the heart of Jesus' teaching and ministry. Also, there are some common denominators in the stories that assist us in drawing some conclusions about what happens when Jesus forgives. This enables us to discern the shaping power of the indwelling Christ who continues to forgive.

It is important to note that Jesus takes the initiative. He invited himself home with Zacchaeus. He asked Simon to take him out in the boat, then instructed him to go farther out to fish again, and followed up his confession with a call. He offered another alternative to the woman already condemned by law for her adultery—even before the woman expressed repentance. The woman at Simon's house was truly penitent, deeply sorry for her sins, but probably held no hope for forgiveness. She does not ask for forgiveness; Jesus offers that gift to her. If that was the

pattern of his ministry and teaching—initiating forgiveness—there is absolutely no reason for anyone of us to go to
bed any night with a conscience in turmoil; no need for us to
spend another day torn apart inside because we feel
separated from God; no reason why we should remain
"lost," out of place, away from home; we are accepted.
Jesus initiates forgiveness. The indwelling Christ is a
forgiving presence.

What a reality to celebrate! Could it be that none of the
persons in the stories I have recalled ever asked to be
forgiven because none of them felt they *deserved* forgiveness? Can it be that, for that same reason, many of us
continue to be debilitated by unrelieved guilt, impotent and
anguishing over severed relationships—we know we don't
*deserve* forgiveness? What a grace in our life: the indwelling
Christ taking the initiative, speaking that word of forgiveness to any who will listen, providing that restorative act for
all who will receive!

Doris Donnelly has written the most helpfully practical
book on forgiveness I know. In *Learning to Forgive* she writes
primarily from the perspective of our need to forgive others
and the power such forgiving provides us. She presents
Jesus as the model of forgiveness, quoting Hannah Arendt
who claimed that "the discoverer of the role of forgiveness
in the realm of human affairs was Jesus of Nazareth." After
making the point that I have just made—that Jesus always
took the initiative in forgiveness—Donnelly closes her book
by talking about what happens when Jesus forgives. Her
outline is so clear I borrow it here.

In forgiving us Jesus *confers self-esteem and self-worth*.
Remember—Christ is an affirming presence. In all the
stories we have shared from the New Testament it is crystal
clear that Jesus refused to connect persons unbindingly
with their sin. He did not deal with them as though their
sins defined who they were, or as though their sins had the
last word in describing or defining their potential. He

offered another alternative, a new possibility. Forgiveness and love had a more powerful and creative word, and was destiny-changing.

That leads to a second thing. In forgiving us Jesus *deals decisively with sin.* Jesus incarnated the promise of the psalmist that God will "remember our sins no more." In Paul's language, our sins are "nailed on the cross," covered over, dissolved, made as nothing by the blood of Christ. Even before the cross, this is made clear in the way Jesus dealt with Zacchaeus and Simon Peter, the woman in Simon's house and the one caught in adultery. The past is gone, over and done with, and will have no influence or power in affecting Jesus' relationship to us now.

How difficult it is, almost impossible, for us to trust that fact! We continue to fall back into the snare of guilt over past sin and failure, continue to be powerless in our self-condemnation and in our refusal to forgive others. We allow our neurotic need to be deserving of what we receive to rob us of the full grace of Jesus' forgiveness. So, by practice—by deliberate attention and response to the indwelling Christ—we gradually come to the experience of freeing forgiveness which can be ours in an ongoing way because we grow in our certainty that Jesus, by forgiveness, deals decisively with sin.

A part of this decisively dealing with sin is that in forgiving *Jesus cancels debt.* It does us no good to get entangled in questions and debate about who owes the debt and to whom is the debt to be paid. To do so is to be victimized by what someone has labeled the "paralysis of analysis." What we do know is that life is pervaded with the principle of payment for deeds done. We talk about criminals paying their "debt to society." We also know that there is a pervading bent in our nature that something has to be done, some payment or adjustment made, to release the offender from the offense. Nathaniel Hawthorne's *The Scarlet Letter* is the classic portrayal of the requirement of payment or debt owed for past sins. Hester Prynne is condemned to wear the scarlet letter as an acknowledgment of her adulterous behavior and the debt she owed an unforgiving community.

In chapter 1 I shared the meaning of the Greek word *prographein* which Barclay translates *placarded*—a word used to describe what a father did when he posted a public notice that he would no longer be responsible for his son's debts. I made the point there that the cross conveys precisely the opposite—that our eternal Father, through his crucified Son, has paid our debts. That is what forgiveness does. The Greek word *aphienai*, which we translate "to forgive," may be actually rendered "to dismiss" or "to release."

There is no more "owing" when Christ forgives. The "debt" is canceled. We are free, loved extravagantly by an eternal Father who forgives. The indwelling Christ keeps reminding us of this fact of our being. As we cultivate an awareness of his presence and yield ourselves to his shaping power, the startling mystery of God's forgiveness keeps exploding within us, spilling out to shape our relationship with others.

That leads to a final fact: in forgiving Jesus *shifts the emphasis from us to God.* What happens as we accept the forgiveness of Christ is that the center of our attention moves from self to God. As Donnelly says, we are moved to focus on the One

who chooses, in the face of our history of infidelity, to affirm, to treasure, and to care for us. That level of forgiveness transfigures. . . .

Jesus neither announces the depravity of the person nor a preoccupation with the past, but rather a prodigal love for his creatures and a looking forward to a future of forgiveness. (*Learning to Forgive*)

Such a shift of attention is kept alive by the indwelling Christ, shaping us, but also as we will discuss in chapter 8, impacting our relationship with others.

## A Healing Presence

There is a close relationship between the forgiving and
healing ministry of Jesus. Even so, we must talk specifically
about *the indwelling Christ as a healing presence.* Mark tells a
story (2:1-12) that makes real the intimate link between
forgiveness and healing. The man in the story, the recipient
of Jesus' forgiveness and healing, was a paralytic. The
picture is at once pathetic and hopeful, tragic and heroic.
You are introduced to a "victim," one immobilized, carried
about on a stretcher. Yet, he has friends, courageous and
hopeful friends, who won't cease believing that there is
help. They are bold in their pursuit of healing—bursting
through the ceiling of the house where Jesus is teaching in
order to get their sick comrade into Jesus' presence.

What happened then astounded those present as it may
astound us if we give it thought. Jesus, seeing the faith of
the man and the four fellows who brought him, announced
to the paralytic, "My son, your sins are forgiven" (Mark
2:5). *What is going on here?* the men must have thought. *We
didn't bring him here to have his sins absolved. Why, the poor
fellow can't walk. We want him up and out of that stretcher.* They
must have also been deeply puzzled, as were others in
the crowd, and shocked at the blasphemy of such an
announcement, "Who can forgive sins but God?" (v. 7).

The interesting fact is that no one doubted what was
going on; the question had to do with who was doing it.
Knowing that, Jesus completed his act of mercy and
affirmed his self-awareness, making clear his mission. He
healed the paralytic. Mark records that Jesus explained his
reason for doing this. "Why must you argue like this in your
minds? Which do you suppose is easier—to say to a
paralysed man, 'Your sins are forgiven,' or 'Get up, pick up
your bed and walk'? But to prove to you that the Son of Man
has full authority to forgive sins on earth, I say to
you,"—and here he spoke to the paralytic—"Get up, pick
up your bed and go home" (vv. 8-11 Phillips).

The fellow sprang to his feet, picked up his bed and walked away, leaving no doubt about the power of Jesus to forgive and heal.

That Jesus connected physical and spiritual disease in a cause-effect fashion may be doubted. But there is no room to doubt that he connected forgiveness and healing, or that there is a connection between our spiritual health and our physical and mental well-being. For that reason we talk about the indwelling Christ as a *healing presence*.

James K. Wagner has written a rather definitive book on how to have an intentional healing ministry in the church. He entitled it *Blessed to Be a Blessing*. Just before the book was published Jim "happened" to see a painting by my wife, Jerry, and was captivated by it, as many have been. He asked that it be used as the cover for his book on healing. I understand why he did that. The painting is an impressionistic design of color and movement, dominantly blue from deep shades to translucent light. The person in the painting, faintly outlined and colored, is not obvious at a glance, but is distinct and focal when really seen. The person stands in the swirl of color and movement surrounded by light and life that is beyond; yet you know that it is this power that is energizing and giving the person life. So, Jim requested and got this painting as the cover for his book.

Jerry called her painting "Grace" and wrote this about it for *Blessed to Be a Blessing*:

In this painting, I have sought to express my experience of God's love as stated in the hymn "I Sought the Lord." One day I was overwhelmed by the realization that while I sought the Lord, all along he was seeking me.

I sought the Lord, and afterward I knew
He moved my soul to seek him, seeking me;
It was not I that found, O Savior true;
No, I was found of thee.

Thou didst reach forth thy hand and mine enfold;
    I walked and sank not on the storm-vexed sea;
'Twas not so much that I on thee took hold
    As thou, dear Lord, on me.

I find, I walk, I love, but oh, the whole
    Of love is but my answer, Lord, to thee!
For thou wert long beforehand with my soul;
    Always thou lovedst me.

Though I was not thinking of healing when I did this painting, I am delighted that it is being used on the cover of this book. The ministry of healing is a manifestation of the grace and power of God's love in our lives.

The painting captures the moment of my response to God's love, which is always a healing experience.

Jim's selection of Jerry's painting *Grace,* for the cover of his book on healing, I believe was intuitive. I doubt if he has reflected or needs to reflect upon why he did it. I have reflected upon it, and I believe there is a deep connection between what Jerry was trying to say about grace in her painting, and what Jim was trying to say about suffering and healing in his writing. It *is* true: our response to God's love is always a healing experience, and the indwelling Christ keeps that love alive in our lives. That is what grace is all about.

Perhaps the best way to put this into perspective quickly is to share some meditative thoughts from *The Workbook of Intercessory Prayer,* which I put down on paper during my recuperation from an awful auto accident. The experience was quite a trauma, physically, mentally, and, to a marked degree, spiritually. A kind of summing up of my ordeal came one day in this prayer.

Lord, it seems as though you've decided
    to keep vivid signs for me
I suppose you know how gullible and
    fickle I am.

Seeing is always believing for me
   Maybe you know I don't always see clearly
   and signs are often misread by me.
   I read more of me than you into them.
So, I've quit putting out fleeces
   and I just struggle to believe
   I keep on waiting—and trusting—
      and longing.
Well, Lord, thank you
   Thank you big;
You've confirmed my waiting and trusting
   and longing
   Not with a sign
   But with your presence
   Your vivid presence.
You have "tented" with me
   for days
The nightmare of a head-on collision
   broken leg, broken ribs, pierced lung
   has been transformed into an incredible
   experience of peace and quietness and
   confidence and knowing.
The miracle has been my consciousness of
   your healing presence
What a miracle that is.
I'd like to build a tabernacle here on
   Mt. Tabor, Lord,
   even with this clumsy leg cast and
   aching muscles and painful breathing.
But I remember some others who wanted to
   stay on Mt. Tabor
   You wouldn't let them
   And you won't let me
You even took them to Gethsemane.
   How different from Mt. Tabor!
I know that when we build permanent temples

where you have been with us in
temporary tents
We don't "house" you
We only box ourselves in.
I won't do that
But I won't forget our "tenting" together
And when my insatiable longing for a
sign wells up again
I'll fight the temptation to put out
a fleece
And will remember our Mt. Tabor.

It was in this experience of suffering and the awareness of a healing presence in the midst of my pain and doubt, my physical immobility and dependency on others, that I realized the intimate connection between suffering and grace. I now join Samuel Miller in wondering why grace has been so dissociated from suffering in theology.

To be sure, [grace] is full of joy, a supernal joy of amazing buoyancy and light; and yet I think that grace and suffering must be seen together. It is by grace that the world of nature is redeemed, and there is no redemption except by the cross. No poem is written, no picture painted, no music made, no sinner forgiven, no child born, no man loved, no truth known, no stone shaped, no peace attained, except grace took a risk, bore a burden, absorbed the evil, and suffered the pain. (*The Dilemma of Modern Belief*)

So the healing presence is not always the dramatic healing of physical or mental disorder to which we can give witness, though sometimes it is. And the healing is not always instantaneous and complete, though there has been such. Most often, healing is a process. The indwelling Christ moves into every area of our life which we open to him, to provide transformation and healing. Not only physically, but perhaps in even more important ways, Christ heals. To the degree of our willingness and openness and yieldedness, we are healed of bitterness, hatred, painful memories, wounded spirits, sores of the soul kept open and infected by estrangement from loved ones, the ravaging grief of a broken heart because of the death of a loved one, the despondency that has come from vocational failure, the frozen will that has come from defeat.

This kind of healing usually takes time. Again Samuel Miller enunciates two truths about God which, if we hold to them, will save us from despair and continue to renew our patience and hope. God "is most certain in the deepest mystery; though He grants no information, He does give His presence. And secondly, we never see Him directly; He is always mediated by the very things that seem to deny Him."

I began this chapter talking about my ministry through short-term encounters, the books I have written, and my correspondence. Recently I received a letter from a woman who expressed her appreciation for my *Workbook of Living Prayer*, and the sustaining healing presence of God that was hers during a particular period that coincided with her use of the *Workbook*. She witnesses clearly to the healing power of the indwelling Christ.

Dear Maxie,

This is my third time to go through *Workbook of Living Prayer* with a group. This time the daytime Lenten Study was with a group of about thirty-five who committed to using the workbook. . . . All of us have found it a rich and rewarding time. . . .

My own most rewarding day in the workbook was day three of the second week. My twenty-three-year-old son was killed in a tragic and sudden manner twenty minutes after he left home to go to work. He hit a bridge, immediately after he hit the bridge he ran and jumped in front of an oncoming vehicle. The strange way he died made it impossible to say accident, and impossible to say suicide. At any rate we were numb with the shock and we went suddenly & instantly from Shrove Tuesday to the other side of Easter. Twelve days later was day three of the second week. When Scott died I had a plane ticket to Atlanta to take my mother from the hospital and bring her here to stay with us to see if she could regain her strength. This trip had been postponed and I went to get her on March 12th. Her health was very, very poor and I felt she would never be able to go back to her home in Atlanta. The move would be hard for her and hard for us. I sat outside in the parking lot and prayed that God would give me wisdom and gentleness, and I prayed for her, for whatever changes would be before us. I spoke aloud the words at the bottom of page 33 "God will sustain me in this situation. No matter what happens he is going to sustain me."* I went up to mother's room and found her dead. Her body was still with some warmth and the nurse had been with her just ten minutes earlier. I, myself, had talked to her about thirty minutes earlier.

Of course my grief and loss is great. This is a troubled time. Still, in these dark days I have had God's peace and presence with me.

To be alive in Christ is to be alive in the world, bearing its sin, its shame, its grief, and its agony. The indwelling Christ is a healing presence, even in the midst of sin, shame, grief, and agony. In him we know what we are doing and what the outcome will be, for his resurrection is our daily hope and glory.

---

*The suggestion given in the *Workbook* for making prayer real during the day to which she refers is as follows:
*During the day*
Think now of the most difficult situation you might encounter today. It may be a task to perform, a personal encounter you anticipate, a decision you must make. Say *aloud* now, "God will be with me in that situation. No matter what happens, he is going to sustain me." When you approach that situation, remind yourself of this fact and remember the promise of the verse upon which you have been meditating: "They that wait upon the Lord. . . ."

# 6

## *A Guiding and Creating Presence*

$A$ friend wrote me about her involvement with a prayer group, using another book of mine, *The Workbook of Intercessory Prayer*. She expressed her appreciation for the book which she called a tool that seemed to come at precisely the right time, and wrote of her joy in the supportive fellowship of her friends and the direction she was finding in prayer. It was no all-is-easy and all-is-clear kind of witness, but rather a grappling with reality in the context of certain faith. Here is a part of her letter.

I would be less than truthful if I didn't say that it is a very difficult time for the Whitakers. We are still dealing with the trauma of Whit's loss of his job—the anger, the resentment, the "Why us?" rises in us from time to time like some kind of specter that will not die. It is just here that you helped me so tremendously. As I learn to use prayer not only as an access to my Father but as a *defense* against "the forces that would destroy his loving plan" for my life. When the negatives begin to surface, it is then that I am able to turn them over to him and overcome destructive forces in my life. I feel so often that I am in the midst of an unfolding drama, sometimes busy as a participant in it, very involved in my part, then again as an observer watching the whole thing with a sense of objectivity. *Very* strange, *very* exciting, very *scary*. I feel caught up in some kind of cosmic event much larger than I am but involving me personally and explicitly. All of this does not always make sense to me, but I am very aware that there is purpose and order to it and that God is using all of this to create in me something very worthwhile. It is what I prayed at the beginning and in that sense I am very much tuned in to the fact that God is not going to waste any of this. This is very philosophical and deeper than I normally try to share, but with you somehow it seems easy.

On the practical side, we struggle with the financial part of it, the tendency to self-pity, the desire to throw in the towel and give up. Decisions are hard to make and what is the worst is that sometimes we find that our anger is directed at *each other*. When that happens, and we catch it, thank God we can say "I'm sorry" and go on. Pray for us, Maxie. Particularly now Whit needs reassurance of his worth as a person, and we need patience to wait upon the Lord.

My friend is convinced that, despite the pain, frustration, and confusion of her present situation, God is guiding, and that "God is using all of this to create in me something very worthwhile." She knows, as I want to affirm in this chapter, that the indwelling Christ is *a guiding and creating presence*.

There may be little distinction between guiding and creating in the way the indwelling Christ shapes our lives, but I think it will add clarity to our thinking to look first at these concepts separately, then to consider them together.

If we don't know where we are going, and if we don't have guidance, our lives become a series of cul-de-sacs, blind alleys, and we are constantly bashing our heads on the proverbial brick wall. There is a funny story about a cowboy that speaks to our normal patterns. He was camping out on the prairie. When it came time to cook breakfast, he could find no kindling or firewood. Bright as he was, he decided to light the grass and hold his skillet over the flame. A wind came up, so he moved along with the fire, holding his skillet over it. This worked fine except that when his eggs were finally cooked, he was three miles from his coffee.

A parable of life. The winds of the world blow and would take the fire of our life in all directions. Likewise, the wind of the spirit blows, and, as Jesus said, we may not know from where it comes or where it goes, but we hear it and we feel it.

We need to learn to distinguish between the wind of the world and the wind of the Spirit. In his conversation with Nicodemus about being born again, Jesus said, "Flesh gives birth to flesh and spirit gives birth to spirit" (John 3:6 Phillips). This is the distinction Paul made between "flesh" and "spirit" which we will consider again in the next chapter. "For those who live according to the flesh set their minds on the things of the flesh, but those who live according to the Spirit set their minds on the things of the Spirit" (Rom. 8:5).

The indwelling Christ is a guiding presence. Some months ago I was leading two retreats for United Methodist Women in West Virginia. It was one of the most exciting and meaningful experiences of this sort I have known. The women there have to have two retreats, back to back, to accommodate those who respond. There were four hundred in each retreat, all open and excited, with a tradition of great things happening each year in these settings, the sort of mood of anticipation and responsiveness that evokes the best in a leader.

I had prepared well, and felt led in my preparation. Yet as I began one of the sessions, I felt a strong urge, a kind of overpowering impulse to talk about something that was not a part of my planning. For the most part, I have learned to follow such leadings. Sometimes I don't, and I'm usually sorry in retrospect. I followed that day and the response was electric. There was a resonance of spirit, a kind of unanimous "yeah." People were convicted and challenged. They responded. I felt the leading was right. I knew it was the guiding presence of the indwelling Christ.

I hesitate to share this because it may appear boastful, certainly less than modest. Yet I run the risk to make the point. In a letter from the chairperson of the retreats a week afterward, there were these two sentences: "You were brilliant, saying all the right things at the right time. You have made yourself available to God and he is using you in a mighty way."

Though extravagant in her assessment, her second sentence was the counterbalance for the first. I am not brilliant, but I do know that in that situation I made myself available to God, I responded to the indwelling Christ, and he used me.

The indwelling Christ is a guiding presence. Any one of us can call from our memory occasions when we knew for certain that we were being guided. But how much of the time do we live in anxiety, uncertain about the direction in which we should go, immobilized by choices, impotent in the presence of opportunity because we are indecisive? We need guidance and we can't lay hold of it.

There are great decisions in life—vocation, marriage, career movement, crisis situations—when our need for guidance is vividly pronounced. But what plagues us most and drains us of so much energy are the intersections upon which we come every day, when we have to choose which way to go. To be sure, we need guidance at the major intersections of our lives, but we need it also at the little crossings and turnings of which our lives primarily consist. My plea is that we see guidance not as episodic, but as an ongoing dynamic which shapes our beings and thus determines decisions and directions.

The guidance of the indwelling Christ is consistent and ongoing. This does not mean that there are not specific times when we seek explicit guidance in particular situations. It does mean that through prayer and other spiritual disciplines we seek to cultivate the awareness of the indwelling Christ to the point that we are delivered from a frantic disposition of mind and heart in the face of decision. We do not come "cold turkey" to a minor or a major crisis. We have the inner sense of Christ's presence. Calling upon that presence, direction is often so clear that the right decision does not even require deciding.

Prayer is crucial in the process, especially an understanding of prayer that makes a big part of it *recognizing and cultivating an awareness of the indwelling Christ*. Christian prayer is characteristically a way of seeking to bring our wills into harmony with God's will. Yet, prayer is often distorted, even by Christians, as an effort to bring God's power to bear upon the accomplishment of our will. We decide what is right and good, then we beseech God to bring it about, or at least help us accomplish it. Though the difference between these two approaches may seem subtle in theory, in practice they are often glaringly at odds. In Christian prayer we seek to orient ourselves to the divine picture of the world. We seek God's perspective—to see ourselves, our problems, our possibilities, our suffering, our dreams through the eyes of Christ.

It is precisely at this point that we must distinguish Christian spirituality from other forms of spirituality. John Cobb makes this point clearly as he calls for our spirituality to be more inherently and essentially integrated with the concern about what is happening in the world, rather than becoming privatistic. I quote him extensively because he makes the point so well.

Taking prayer as the center of what's often thought of as spirituality, we have to ask what is the distinctive character of Christian prayer. I assume the Lord's Prayer is as normative for understanding Christian prayer as anything could be. We ask ourselves the question, "What is really going on if we genuinely pray, 'Thy kingdom come, thy will be done.'" That is a very political prayer. The function of the prayer is that through praying it we come to orient ourselves toward what we are praying for.

I'm interested in oriental religions. I think the influence of oriental notions of spirituality has cut in the opposite direction of what I advanced authentic Christian spirituality to be. It's not that it's impractical, if I can take zen as an example. Zen enables one to perform whatever functions come one's way better than one could without the discipline of zen. It's eminently practical, but doesn't introduce any distinctive judgement upon which practices are the appropriate ones. A pianist can play the piano better and a samurai can be a better swordsman through the practice of zen. Zen is not a way of deciding whether or not one should be a swordsman or a pianist. That's quite different from biblical spirituality, where the

primary focus seems to be upon aligning one's will with the will of
God. Presumably God's will is not primarily directed to the
excellence with which I perform my daily round. I don't mean to
exclude that, but it isn't what I get from the Old and New
Testaments as the primary focus. . . .

I don't think we understand the will of God properly in terms of
any set of rules. That would be law rather than spirit. My
translation of aligning my will with God's will is a transformation
of point of view, to see the world or to think of the world more as
God sees it and thinks of it. With respect to all the decisions of life,
instead of asking the question if I can afford something, I'm asking
whether God favors it, but that's also whether the world can afford
it. I don't read the newspapers and ask how beneficial certain
developments are for my class, my race, my nation, whatever, but
rather how this is affecting life on this planet in the most
comprehensive sense. (*Haelan*, Spring 1981)

The transformation of a point of view which Dr. Cobb
says is at the heart of prayer—"aligning my will with
God's"—for me as a Christian is accomplished by the
indwelling Christ. The more vivid my awareness of this
presence, the more clearly I understand the nature and
character of this presence, the more confidently can I
experience guidance, and the more certain I can be that my
life is being aligned with God's will.

We will speak more of this in chapter 8. For now, we need
to note briefly that as we cultivate the presence of the
indwelling Christ we discover that he guides us through
persons and through events.

I suggested at the close of chapter 1 that as we come alive
in Christ, we can be Christ to and/or receive Christ from
every person we meet. Often I will begin a retreat by having
persons share a love greeting. I ask them to select some one
they don't know very well or not at all, get the person's first
name, and exchange a greeting in this fashion. In pairs, they
stand facing each other, holding both hands of each other,
looking each other directly in the eye, and saying, "Mary,
the love of Jesus in me greets the love of Jesus in you, and
brings us together in the name of the Father, the Son, and

the Holy Spirit." Then the other person shares the same greeting. I instruct them ahead of time to sit quietly after each has shared the greeting, without any comment, reflecting on what they are feeling. It is amazing how the mood changes. It is not unusual to see tears in people's eyes and have persons witness to a vivid awareness of the presence of Christ.

To be sure, this is in a special setting, but it at least suggests an ever-present possibility. John A. T. Robinson said, "The Christian cannot look into a human face without seeing Jesus and cannot look into Jesus' face without seeing God." The more we cultivate our awareness of the indwelling Christ, the more we resonate to his aliveness in others and discern his guidance through them. Also, the more sensitive we are to his presence, the more perceptive we are to the pain and need of others which present calls to our lives.

It interests me the way some people talk about knowing Jesus *personally*. With many, it is altogether too limited—a *me-and-Jesus spiritual intimacy* that seems to have never heard Jesus' word about what knowing him *personally* means: "If you have fed someone, clothed someone, visited someone in prison, given someone shelter . . . you have loved me."

Through persons, and also through events and circumstances the indwelling Christ guides us. A character in one of Dostoevski's novels says, "There's a new man in me. A new man being born in me, but the new man would not have been born if God had not sent the storm."

That's a serious expression of it. A humorous expression of it is the story about a rich Texas rancher who threw a party for all his friends.

For the entertainment at the party, he filled his Olympic-size swimming pool with sharks. In the course of the evening, he invited the guests to stand around the pool while he announced that if any young man would jump in and swim across the pool, he would give him one of three things: "you may have my ranch, or a million dollars, or the hand of my daughter in marriage." A commotion at the other end of the pool claimed everyone's attention. One man had jumped in and frantically swam across the pool, fighting off the sharks in the churning, boiling water. Miraculously he made it to the other side safely and the rancher was dumbfounded. "I didn't think any one would take me up on that offer, but I'm a man of my word. What do you want? You can have one of three choices—my ranch, a million dollars, or you can have my daughter's hand in marriage." The man said, "I don't want any of those things." Shocked even more, the rancher said, "All right, you name it and I'll get it for you." The man said, "I want the guy that shoved me into the pool."

We do get thrown into situations we don't want to be in. We are often submerged in circumstances beyond our control. Things we have planned and counted on never materialize. Dreams turn to dust and ambitions become ashes. In and through all of these the indwelling Christ can guide us. It is difficult in the midst of some of these events and circumstances to perceive that guidance is taking place. Yet in retrospect we can see that there was something providential happening. In my friend's words with which I began this chapter, we become "very aware that there is purpose and order to it and that God is using all of this to create in me something very worthwhile."

## A Creating Presence

The indwelling Christ is *a creating presence*.

From November 20, 1980, to February 15, 1981, at the Hirshorn Museum in Washington, D.C., there was an art show billed "The Avant Garde in Russia—1910-1930: New Perspectives." During a visit to Washington I stumbled upon the show and was glad I did. Though I am not sophisticated in my understanding, I appreciate art. Even with my limited understanding, I could sense in that show the art revolution that had accompanied the political, economic, and social revolution of Russia during those years. No aspect of art was left unchallenged. Traditional concepts about painting, sculpture, photography, graphic and decorative arts, theatrical, industrial and costume design were all scrutinized, and often rejected.

It was during that period, in 1924, that George Balanchine, the world's greatest choreographer, escaped to the West. Since then, interrupted only by World War II, a steady stream of Russian ballet dancers, including such brilliant notables as Valery and Galine Ponous, and the most celebrated of our time, Mikhail Baryshnikov, have followed Balanchine's example.

These left for artistic reasons. They defected not primarily for political reasons, but because the political system would not allow them to develop their art to its utmost. The system was too restrictive, too confining. They wanted the freedom to dance.

At the show of the Avant-Garde in Russia in Washington, I picked up a newsprint broadside which described the art. One full page contained quotations from artists of the period. One, from Vladimir Markov (1912), gives the reason for the stream of defections from Russia, but is also a description of who we are: "The aspiration to other worlds is inherent in man's nature. Man does not want to walk, he demands dancing; he does not want to speak, he demands song; he does not want the earth but strains toward the sky."

So we do. One of the great discoveries of my life is that the indwelling Christ is a presence that stimulates, empowers, even directs the creative thrust of my spirit. When I dedicate the gifts God has given me to him, when I am willing to turn loose, as it were, and allow the Spirit to flow, I am amazed at what happens. The indwelling Christ is a creating presence. I see myself as a rather disciplined person, at least in most areas. I am disciplined in my study, disciplined in work schedules, disciplined in my attention to family relations and responsibilities, somewhat disciplined in my devotional life. I am a diligent worker and believe work is an important part of the life process. I am certain, however, that the energizing vitality for what comes from my life these days is from the creating presence of the indwelling Christ.

One bit of personal sharing will illustrate. I came to The Upper Room in 1973 as a staff person to work in the area of prayer and spiritual renewal. No one was quite certain about the specific shape of my responsibility, only that there was a great need in inspiring, motivating, and providing resources for persons to discover and sustain a vital life of prayer. I accepted this responsibility, not because I felt I was capable or had any expertise in the field. In fact, I said to Dr. Weldon, the editor of *The Upper Room*, and Dr. Galloway, the general secretary of the Board of Evangelism, that the very fact that they were interviewing me for such a responsibility showed what desperate straits the church was in. I accepted the responsibility because this was my own felt need and the growing edge of my life, and I was convinced that the church was in desperate need for the revitalization that could come from prayer and a renewal of spirituality.

Spirituality was a vague and disfavored word. No one I knew in Protestant Christianity was talking about "spiritual formation." When I rather timidly started using the term, raised eyebrows and blank facial puzzlement were the normal responses. It did not help that I was unfamiliar with the literature in the field and could not call on my own Protestant Christian tradition and literature to support my convictions and commitment.

These years, first as a staff person and now as editor, responsible for all the exciting, worldwide ministries of The Upper Room, have been the most meaningful of my life. What I deem my most important contribution during this period is a result of the creating presence of the indwelling Christ.

Early after beginning my work at The Upper Room, it became clear to me that one of the most obvious needs of persons was to learn to pray. As a pastor I had made the mistake that pastors continue to make: we assume people know how to pray. We call them to pray, exhort them to pray, preach convincingly about the power of prayer—never recognizing that even people who are convinced of prayer's validity and want to pray don't know how.

I read much of the great literature in prayer, especially from the Protestant perspective. I was reminded again of the theology of prayer and the biblical teaching about prayer. And many of these great books offered "ways" to pray. What could I do to add to such a great literature? Or, what could I do to make that literature available to people? I struggled and strained, burdened by what I felt was a genuine call to help people in the whole concern of finding and sustaining a life of prayer.

I remember the occasion when a breakthrough came—though I can label it as a breakthrough only in retrospect. I was in a silent retreat at Dayspring, the retreat center of The Church of The Saviour in Washington, D.C. I had never been much for silence. It was a threat, not a joyful invitation to me. But those I admired and from whom I had learned so much stressed the value of silence as a spiritual discipline and as a vital source of renewal. I had begun to test the idea and was in that retreat seeking to cultivate an openness to the meaning silence could have in my life.

The only instruction the retreat leader had given was, "Just let go. Don't try to manufacture anything, don't anticipate anything specific happening." Well, I didn't, and it didn't. It was a boring, exasperating twenty-four hours. I couldn't relax and I couldn't let go. I couldn't give up the thought that I was "over my head" in a responsibility for which I was at best ill-equipped, and at worst a very poor model of what vital prayer is all about.

Toward the end of that ponderous twenty-four hours, which I thought would perhaps never come to a close, during which I nightmarishly thought I might be caught forever in silence with no one with whom I could talk, I had this uncanny feeling—almost a releasing, relaxing sort of floating feeling; near words—though not clear and audible—which left a certainty in my mind. The certainty was that a breakthrough was going to come, if I would simply trust the Spirit.

That was enough to go on. During the weeks that followed, the plan and organization for *The Workbook of Living Prayer* began to form itself in my mind. Within four or five months it was completed.

There is nothing unique about the content of that book. You can find most of it, in essence, in a lot of other books. But the dynamic of it is that it is a workbook, and that people who actually use it find themselves involved in a process that is energizing, even life-changing. That is unique, and it was all gift. I like to say that you cannot use the workbook without actually praying, because the engagement in the use of the workbook is an engagement in prayer. Almost daily a letter or some personal word comes to me confirming this. Nothing I have ever done, in my judgment, has had this sort of meaningful impact upon so many. I am certain that the *Workbook* was a gift of the Spirit, the indwelling Christ working creatively in me.

My wife, Jerry, is an artist with much less formal training than most artists, but with a great reservoir of natural gifts. She is very deliberate about allowing the creating presence of the indwelling Christ to work within her. Her meditation/prayer experience is very explicit. She immerses herself in Scripture that affirms the love, concern, and power of Christ at work within her. She makes three specific petitions. One, that she will be open to Christ's creative inspiration and guidance. Two, that she will be led to the resources to equip her for the task—either her past learning, training and experience, or persons or resources who can be helpful in that particular task. Three, that she will love and trust herself and what comes from her designing, painting, and drawing, confident to express herself as well as possible, then in her words, "let it go."

The third movement in her preparation is a kind of meditation. Having immersed herself in affirmation from Scripture, and having prayed very specifically, she relaxes for twenty or thirty minutes, awake but in an almost-sleep, she empties herself in order to receive what Christ has to offer. From that relaxed receptivity, she proceeds with her work. She is confident that the indwelling Christ works creatively within her. Knowing her—her long, arduous battle with deep feelings of inadequacy and low self-esteem—I am convinced that this is the saving dynamic of her life—the creating presence of the indwelling Christ.

Do not mistake what I am saying. We are gifted in many different ways, each person uniquely so. We are endowed with talents and natural gifts. Apart from natural endowments the Holy Spirit also gives specific and different gifts to different people. Paul's word is applicable in either case: "The gifts we possess differ as they are allotted to us by God's grace, and must be exercised accordingly" (Rom. 12:6 NEB). The likelihood of my ever painting like Jerry, or Jerry writing a workbook on prayer is rare—but the indwelling Christ works creatively in each of us.

In 1963 Jerry and I had the privilege of visiting East Africa. The treasures we brought home were two wood carvings, magnificent examples of the sculptors' art. We knew nothing of the art, but were moved by the feeling tone, even the story told by each piece. These individually carved pieces are not easily found today, but happily there are those keeping the art alive. Long after finding our "treasures," I read René Dubos' word about the primitive wood sculptors of Africa who make those magnificent carvings. He said they first carefully select the fragment of wood they are going to use, from a limb, or the trunk of a tree, or even a root. They not only look for soundness in the wood, they scrutinize the shape and grain, the pattern of the structures of the wood. The carver does not impose a shape upon the wood; he believes its natural form is already there and he lets the wood be what it is. The wood sculptors believe there is a spirit in the wood; the wood has a life of its own which the sculptor helps give expression to. Our two carvings reflect that. One a tall strong figure carrying a great burden, but resolute and determined. The other a figure crouched low, only the head prominent, brooding, the wisdom of the ages stirring within his mind. The primitive artists working with their wood is a parable of the indwelling Christian as a creative presence.

E. Stanley Jones had the capacity to put profound truths in brief, pithy statements. Many of these, at first hearing or reading, were shocking and the immediate response was challenge or argument. That is what made him such a powerful communicator all over the world. One of his favorite themes was "To be most Christian is to be most natural." On the surface that goes against the grain of our typical thinking about fallen human nature.

But Brother Stanley was right. To be most Christian is to allow the indwelling Christ to help us become what we are naturally (in creation by God) intended to be. So, we are unique, and our uniqueness is affirmed. Keith Miller's picture of the tragedy of the church, seeking to make itself a trumpet corps instead of seeing itself as an orchestra, is a challenging one. What pathetic tragedy, Keith would say, piccolos trying to play in the tuba section.

Alive in Christ, our rich diversity as persons, our unique gifts are enriched and enhanced by the creating presence. Frederick Herzog stimulated in me the idea that the result of the creating presence of the indwelling Christ is not an *imitation of Christ* which can easily become superficial and counterfeit. It is a creating power which allows free expression and fulfillment of our unique selves. So it is not an *imatatio Christi, imitation of Christ,* but an *innovatio Christi,* an *innovation of Christ,* a fresh expression of Christ through each of us. We will consider this more in chapters 8 and 9.

# 7

## *A Converting Presence*

Kim, my twenty-one-year-old daughter, and I spent a rare couple of hours together in one of those precious exchanges that can never be planned; they can only be entered into when the setting is right, when the dynamic of soul-open-to-soul is sensed and both persons respond, encourage, gently probe, and sensitively listen. You never know, even in retrospect, just how it happened, so you can't devise a formula to make it happen again. You only know that you have been sensitive enough to take off your shoes and walk lightly about on holy ground. Such awareness makes all *meeting* potentially holy, packed with the possibility of being Spirit-infused.

The beginning of Kim's and my holy two hours was triggered I think by her talking about the B she made in a Christian ethics course in her third college year. She thought she deserved an A, but that was not the point. The point was a difference of "starting points" between her and the professor. The final exam was an oral one and this required an extensive personal dialogue with the professor. Kim believes that persons are basically good, that we are created in the image of God, and that no matter what we have done, or how far from that point of beginning we may have wandered or deliberately fled, we are basically good.

Dig deep enough into the core of a person, she would say, and you will discover that which is divine. For Kim, that is the starting point for exploring ethics, especially Christian ethics.

I am not sure of the degree to which her professor disagreed (Kim thought it was a drastic difference—enough to give her a B rather than an A), but his starting point was that experientially in ethics you must begin with the fact that persons are *not* basically good. We are all sinners. The truth is, both Kim and the professor are right. I like Kim's tenacity of conviction, and I like the realism of the professor. Like me, he was schooled in the liberal theology that naïvely failed to reckon with the degree of our *fallenness*. But the holocaust, Vietnam, the assassination of Martin Luther King and bombings and killings that were strewn along the road to human rights for blacks and other minorities in the fifties and sixties—these are too recent in our human history, and too vivid a witness to human depravity, for us to begin at any point but our fallen nature.

Kim's conflict with her professor, and the fact that they are both right, makes what this book is all about so crucial. Recall again a core dimension of the gospel which we discussed in chapter 2. Two things happened in *the fall* and in our *own fall*. One, we became estranged from God; two, God's image within us was broken, distorted, defaced. Kim is right—the image was not destroyed; the basic core of divinity is still there. But we must reckon with the fact that the basic core of divinity is not intact as God's image. Two things happen in salvation. One, we are reconciled to God; our estrangement is dissolved by the justifying grace of God in the cross of Jesus. Two, there is the re-creation of the image of God in the life of the believer. We are born again to begin a *process of new birth*.

The first grade church school class had been talking about the first men Jesus called to be his followers—the disciples. Reviewing the lesson the next Sunday, I asked the children what these first helpers of Jesus were called. There was a long pause, then one child eagerly raised his hand. "The Recycles!" he exclaimed. (Mary Burton, *alive now!* Jan./Feb. 1974)

The child's innocent confusion of words is a telling metaphor of salvation. Recycle is a familiar word to children sensitive to ecology, and may be a powerful hint as to how we might communicate the gospel to them. Isn't the concept in harmony with the gospel promise? Salvation is human souls being *recycled* by God's forgiving love and renewing power in Jesus Christ.

So the final word we speak about the shaping power of the indwelling Christ is that he is a *converting presence.*

It is a commentary on our failure to be clear in communicating the gospel that I struggled for the right word here. *Converting* is a rather specialized word, in religion and other disciplines. It is a common word in physics, chemistry, and engineering—conversion of energy, of materials, of solids to liquids, liquids to solids, gases to fire and heat and cold. Though a common word in religious language, it is not common in usage today, and to a marked degree has lost its power. We have allowed narrow fundamentalists to restrict and distort its meaning. Not being willing to be squeezed into that mold, we have given up one of our most powerful and descriptive words. We have even gone further in many quarters of the church. Not only have we given up the word, we have diminished a cardinal principle of the gospel which the word describes. We simply do not think much within the church about conversion. When we think about it, too often we use it to designate only that beginning point of our salvation when we accept God's gracious love in Jesus Christ and are justified through our faith in God's sacrificial gift of himself for our sins.

The late seventies and early eighties witnessed a resurgence of "evangelical" Christianity. With the election of Jimmy Carter to the presidency, we had a "born again

Christian" in the White House, so the term gained
credence. Again, a word of caution. The popularity of a
word does not always reflect the reality of experience, and
words can be diluted in their meaning. I know why we came
to the point where we began to talk about "born again
Christians." We had churches filled with persons for whom
the transforming power of Jesus Christ had no experiential
reality. Unfortunately, however, "born again Christian"
has become jargon for a type of conversion experience that
in reality marks only the beginning of the Christian life. In
the context of the gospel, to use the term "born again" to
describe a Christian is redundant. To be a Christian *is* to be
born again, and to be born again is to be Christian. As Jesus
said to Nicodemus, this is a *must*, not an option, if we are to
be his followers. And it is not our own doing; it is the Spirit
working in us. We are not saved by our own moral
self-improvement, nor by refining our belief system, nor by
doing and being better and better. We are saved by allowing
God's power of love to work radically within us. The
indwelling Christ is a converting presence, restoring and
renewing that distorted and defaced image of God within
us. We can rightfully speak about being born again because
it is that dramatic. There is in the Christian experience
of salvation a discontinuity between what was and what
now is.

Return to my reflection on my holy two hours with my
daughter Kim. A few days after that conversation, in my
devotional reading I came upon Mark 12:13-17. At any other
time I may not have experienced this passage as a call to
conversion—but my meeting with Kim and the question it
raised was still astir in my mind—*what is our basic nature?*
Traditionally we call upon this passage to teach about
financial stewardship, and that message is there.

The Pharisees and the Herodians teamed up to trap Jesus.
They began with nauseous flattery: "Master, you are an
honest man, . . . and truckle to no one, . . . you teach in all
honesty the way of life that God requires" (Mark 12:14

NEB). Jesus could not be ployed by such superficial baiting. He knew what they were about; still he listened.

Paying taxes was as hot an issue then as now, and popular leaders like Jesus were expected to have a word on the matter. His provocateurs were not really interested in Jesus' opinion on the matter of taxes. They wanted to embarrass and discredit him in public, to diminish his influence by creating confusion and dissension among his followers.

"Are we or are we not permitted to pay taxes to the Roman Emperor?" How crafty their question. Jesus knew. If he said yes, he could be seen as supportive of the pagan Roman rule and a betrayer of Jewish hopes for freedom. His enemies thought they had him in a corner; I can imagine their sly knowing smiles. But a more knowing twinkle lights Jesus' eyes, as he responds, "Why are you trying to trap me? Bring me a coin, and let's look at it. Whose image is this, and whose inscription?" The coin, a denarius, was a silver piece, the most common of Roman money. One denarius was the daily wage for a laborer and the annual census tax levied on every person from ages twelve through sixty-five. On one side was the image of Tiberius, the Roman Emperor. The inscription was "of Tiberius Caesar, the divine Augustus." So, the reply to Jesus' question was self-evident, "Caesar's, of course." But Jesus' response to their answer was not anticipated, for they heard him in astonishment. "Pay Caesar what is due to Caesar, *and pay God what is due to God.*"

And what is due to God? What bears his image? *Ourselves.* It is the claim of Scripture over and over again. "So God created [persons] in his own image." "What is man that thou art mindful of him, . . . Yet thou hast made him a little less than God." "Put on the new nature, created after the likeness of God." "Be perfect, as your heavenly Father is perfect." "The glory which thou [God] hast given me I have given to them, . . . I in them and thou in me." Kim is right. "Here and now, dear friends, we are God's children; what we shall be has not yet been disclosed, but we know that when it is disclosed we shall be like him, because we shall see him as he is" (I John 3:2 NEB).

But how do we get Kim and her professor together? By connecting our beginning word about the shaping power of the indwelling Christ—the affirming Presence—with his work as a converting Presence. They go together. The indwelling Christ affirms our beings as persons. The human creature is good. Who put it in the vernacular? "God made me, and God don't make no trash!" One of the church fathers, Irenaeus, cast it in an unforgettable sentence: "The glory of God is man fully alive."

Our salvation history follows this cycle: good news, bad news, good news. Good news: we were created in the image of God. Bad news: we sinned, rebelled against God; God image within has been fractured and distorted. Good news: we are forgiven by Christ and are being restored in the image of God, transformed into the likeness of Christ.

Unfortunately much of the classic teaching in the area of spiritual formation has focused narrowly on disciplines that were to mortify, suppress, even "kill," some of our basic human drives or attributes. Thus most Christian spirituality prior to the twentieth century has been primarily ascetic. It divided our nature, staging battles between "flesh" and spirit, seeking to cultivate the spirit at the expense of the body. Thus our primary model of spirituality has been the *ascetic* one. Throughout the history of the Roman Catholic Church, the monastic calling has been seen as the highest vocation. Though not as tenaciously held, the idea persists today.

And it is not restricted to the Roman Church. All Christian spirituality has been shaped by the great spiritual classics such as *The Imitation of Christ*. With telling consistency, these classics sought to teach us how to suppress our normal drives and desires and so strengthen the spirit. The Puritan expression of Christianity which has infused all of Protestantism was almost as world denying as monasticism.

In Puritan and ascetic spirituality there was especially an intense negative view of human sexuality. It was as though to be male and female, and all that meant in terms of sexual drive and gratification, was the seedpod of evil. "Original sin" was even linked with our conception as human beings in the act of sexual intercourse. From that conviction it was inevitable that celibacy, the abstinence from all sexual relation, became one of the highest vows in the spiritual life. I am not discounting the spiritual value of celibacy, nor would I deny that celibacy as an aspect of vocation can be an enriching experience, enhancing one's ministry. I'm simply arguing against an understanding of human nature and spirituality that reduces sex to something negative, even evil, and divides persons into warring enemies: body and spirit.

What do we do with the content of Scripture, especially from Paul, that dramatically presents the conflict between "flesh" and "spirit"? We talked about this in chapter 4, but it helps to review for our discussion here. A careful study of Paul's letters reveals the fact that he does not set *flesh* against *spirit*, with flesh being naturally evil and something that we have to destroy. Nor does he equate *flesh* and *body*, making flesh the substance of the body. These are too different words in Greek: *sarx* is flesh, *soma* is body.

Some inconsistencies in translating the New Testament as a result of Greek thought have led to a confusion of meaning. In New Testament times, one strong strand of Greek thought was concerned with the essence of things, thus a preoccupation with the nature of "soul" and its relation to mind and body. This led to a dualism of flesh and spirit, with the emerging perception of an ongoing struggle between the divine Spirit and our bodies, and between our "lower" and "higher" natures. It was the lingering effect of Greek thought that led to the unfortunate translation of Romans 8 where "flesh" becomes "lower nature" in the New English Bible. The whole of Paul leads me to believe that this is precisely what Paul does not mean.

Paul was a Hebrew, rooted in Hebrew thought in which a division of *man* into lower and higher natures was almost wholly absent. In Hebrew thought, *flesh* was not an element of the self at war with some "higher" element; it was the whole of human existence. So you have Isaiah's promise that "the glory of the Lord shall be revealed, and *all flesh* shall see it together" (40:5, italics mine). Following that he says, "All flesh is grass" and withers (v. 6), "but the word of our God will stand for ever" (v. 8). Human life is transient, Isaiah is saying. So I repeat an earlier word: Flesh is not a neutral term describing a "nature" or our "essence." It is an evaluative term describing the transitory, temporary dimensions of our existence, the fact of the weakness, finiteness, and vulnerability of our earthly sojourn. Flesh and sin are not to be equated. Paul contrasts flesh and spirit in describing the way we live. Spirit and flesh are domains of power, spheres of influence in which one lives. Sin is closely linked to flesh because flesh is the domain of power where sin operates. Paul condemns sin, not flesh. God came in Christ to enter the domain of flesh in order that sin might be conquered once and for all.

This understanding and conviction gives clarity to Paul's continuous contention that there was no salvation by *law*. Law operates in the domain of flesh, where we live without the transforming power of the indwelling Christ. In the flesh, we are impotent to keep the law. How vividly real to our own experience is Paul's testimony in Romans 8:1-6 when we read it in this light.

There is therefore now no condemnation for those who are in Christ Jesus. For the law of the Spirit of life in Christ Jesus has set me free from the law of sin and death. For God has done what the law, weakened by the flesh, could not do: sending his own Son in the likeness of sinful flesh and for sin, he condemned sin in the flesh, in order that the just requirement of the law might be fulfilled in us, who walk not according to the flesh but according to the Spirit. For those who live according to the flesh set their minds on the things of the flesh, but those who live according to the Spirit set their minds on the things of the Spirit. To set the mind on the flesh is death, but to set the mind on the Spirit is life and peace. (Rom. 8:1-6)

This is the key that unlocks the door to vital Christian living—the powerful dynamic of *the Spirit of life in Christ Jesus that frees us.* For those who live according to the flesh set their minds on the things of the flesh, but those who live according to the Spirit, set their minds on the things of the Spirit. The perspective is important. Our predicament is not that we are *in the flesh,* but that we want to live *according* to the flesh, that is setting our minds on "the flesh" as a domain of power. Jesus is not at war with our humanity. The destruction of our human nature is not the goal of Christ-living, but conversion—the conversion of our feelings, drives, passions, instincts.

There is no question. When we are honest, most of us readily confess with Paul that there is "a war going on in my members." We *will* to do something, but find ourselves doing just the opposite. For some of us, the inner conflict is a full-scale war. For others, who have been on the way for some time, it may be more like guerrilla warfare, with pockets of enemy forces holding out here and there, moving in for episodic confrontations. This is why we must experience the indwelling Christ as a converting presence and power. Also, we must realize that we need a series of conversions. The new life that has come to birth within us is a process of conversion, through which the power of the indwelling Christ brings all the powers of our being, all the feelings, instincts, drives, and passions into wholeness. These powers are not suppressed or pummeled into subjection; they are focused, coordinated, harnessed—in a word, converted to constructive expressions of our new life in Christ.

To deal with the feelings, drives, instincts, and passions of our life which need to be converted would require at least an entire book. Our love needs converting because love can be perverted. Our sexual drives need converting because sex is too often kept at a base level of animal heat, rather than transformed into an expression of love and self-giving. Our acquisitive instincts need converting because too often this instinct turns into selfish grasping of any and everything we desire. Our instinct for survival needs converting. This is one of our most basic needs and it drives us to hoard our resources, to lock ourselves within ourselves, never becoming vulnerable, never risking self-disclosure, ordering our entire lives after the model of a limited bank account against which we are afraid to draw lest we give out too soon. Pride, without which we often become sluggards or are overcome with self-depreciation, even self-hatred, and with which we often become self-centered egotists, needs converting. What J. Wallace Hamilton labels the "drum-major instinct," needs converting. This is a drive that encompasses many different expressions, most of which are in the forefront of our lives at one time or another. It is a retinue of drives and feelings attendant to the passion *to be first* in line.

I could go on, and so could you, up or down the scale according to who is making the list: the need to belong, the fear of failure, the craving for attention, the passion for security, the obsession for power, the pull of adventure, the lure of mystery, the yearning for community, the longing for intimacy, the lust for sexual satisfaction, the seductive power of glamour, the craving for comfort, and the pull of the familiar.

What do we do with ourselves? How do we deal with these hordes of feelings and passions? We recognize them, and name them if we can. We affirm that they are a part of who we are. They are not evil shoots to be uprooted and cast away, or wild tares foreign to the harvest of a healthy personality. J. Wallace Hamilton in *Ride the Wild Horses!* puts it well:

Jesus is not at war with our human nature. He does not say that our instincts were born of evil or that our only hope is to cast them out, or to beat them down. He understood perfectly, in the realm of human nature, what Luther Burbank discovered in the realm of plant nature: that every weed is a potential flower, and that the very qualities which make it a weed could make it a flower. Great sinners and great saints contain much the same stuff.

The indwelling Christ is a converting presence. This converting aspect of his shaping power is connected with his affirming work. His converting and affirming presence work together to bring wholeness. Every aspect of our being is to be yielded to the converting power of the indwelling Christ. Obviously we are talking about a process that requires time. Recall our working understanding of spiritual formation: the dynamic process of receiving by faith and appropriating through commitment, discipline, and action, the living Christ into our life to the end that our life will conform to, and manifest the reality of Christ's presence in the world. The claim is bold and extravagant— that we can so live with Christ, so cultivate the awareness of his presence within us, and so yield ourselves to his shaping power that we can become new persons, persons who reflect his likeness.

But how? That is the question. And the answer is not simple or easy. Through prayer, if we understand that a big part of prayer is recognizing and cultivating an awareness of the indwelling Christ. And through commitment and the disciplines of spiritual formation by which our lives are conformed to Christ. Paul gives us some direction. "If then you have been raised with Christ, seek the things that are above, where Christ is, seated at the right hand of God. Set your minds on things that are above, not on things that are on earth. For you have died, and your life is hid with Christ in God. When Christ who is our life appears, then you also will appear with him in glory" (Col. 3:1-4).

As we contended in chapter 2, dying and rising with Christ is the rhythm of the Christian life. Prayer and spiritual formation is the deliberate, intentional effort to live

our whole life in the context of the life, death, and
resurrection of Jesus. Our *union* with Christ is in death and
resurrection. Pascal said, "It is one of the greatest principles
of Christianity that that which happened in Jesus Christ
may happen in the soul of the Christian. We have a linking
not only with Calvary, but with his resurrection."
Commitment to Christ is to die to flesh as the domain of
power controlling our lives; that is to die to *our own* control
of our lives. Then we share Christ's resurrection, Christ
lives in us and we experience being raised to a new level of
living *under his guidance and by his power*.

There is a sense in which we are no longer in control, no
longer in charge of our destiny. Sure, we continue to make
decisions and we are always responsible. Yet, the process of
conversion is the process of yielding every aspect of our
lives, every drive, feeling, passion, and instinct, to the
indwelling Christ every day.

There is an interesting phrase in this word of Paul to the
Colossians (3:1-4), simple, easy to pass over, but packed
with meaning: "Christ who is our life." This is no incidental
word for Paul. "It is no longer I who live," he said, "but
Christ who lives in me" (Gal. 2:20). "For to me to live is
Christ" (Phil. 1:21). This claim of Paul to life in Christ is
always connected with death and resurrection. "If we have
been united with him in a death like his, we shall certainly
be united with him in a resurrection like his. . . . consider
yourselves dead to sin and alive to God in Christ Jesus"
(Rom. 6:5, 11). Conversion then, the work of Christ within
us, is the process of death and resurrection, with our
ultimate hope being a final resurrection "when Christ . . .
appears, [and we shall] also . . . appear with him in glory"
(Col. 3:4).

Paul states this hope, then moves on to touch the nerve
endings of all our lives—the fact that we still have thoughts
and feelings, habits and attitudes, ways of relating and a
seductive proneness to sin which mock any claim that
Christ is in us, and *is* our life.

Put to death therefore what is earthly in you: fornication, impurity, passon, evil desire, and covetousness, which is idolatry. On account of these the wrath of God is coming. In these you once walked, when you lived in them. But now put them all away: anger, wrath, malice, slander, and foul talk from your mouth. Do not lie to one another, seeing that you have put off the old nature with its practices and have put on the new nature, which is being renewed in knowledge after the image of its creator. (Col. 3:5-10)

If anyone has had thoughts about conversion being a *fait accompli*, an accomplished reality with our experience of being justified by faith, this passage should at least cause second thoughts. But most of us do not need Scripture to tell us that. I know—how painfully do I know—even as I write this. I am deeply satisfied with the "position" the church has given me to exercise my vocation. I cannot imagine a more meaningful and exciting place for me within the church. Yet, just yesterday a bishop called to talk with me about a "move," and all sorts of feelings and emotions stirred within me. Boiling to the top, and I had to name it, was that "drum-major" instinct—the desire to be recognized, to have status; yes, if I press it honestly, "to sit on the right side."

How presumptuous of me—to write about the indwelling Christ and the transformed, victorious life he brings! How well I know discouragement and defeat that comes from aspects of myself not yet fully yielded to his Lordship. How aware I am of my own impotence to change some things which continue to debilitate me.

Still I write—and boldly! I do so, confident that the crucial battle has been fought and won through the death and resurrection of Christ, and through my death to self and resurrection to new life. I do so, certain that the Holy Spirit will penetrate and occupy every aspect of my being as I recognize and cultivate my awareness of the indwelling Christ.

Here is a parable of the truth from the remarkable musician, Pablo Casals:

Each day I am reborn. Each day I must begin again. For the past 80 years I have started each day in the same manner. It is not a mechanical routine but something essential to my life. I go to the piano and I play two preludes and fugues of Bach. I cannot think of doing otherwise. It is a benediction on the house. But that is not its only meaning for me. It is a rediscovery of the world of which I have the joy of being a part. It fills me with the wonder of eternity, with the incredible miracle of God. The music is never the same for me. Each day is something new, fantastic, unbelievable!

So it is as we yield ourselves to the converting presence of the indwelling Christ. The "music" is never the same, since we have "put off the old nature with its practices and have put on the new nature, *which is being renewed* . . . after the image of its creator" (Col. 3:10, italics mine). It takes time—a lifetime, really—to come to spiritual maturity, to grow up "to the measure of the stature of the fulness of Christ" (Eph. 4:13). But how exciting—to know that it can happen, and to feel the power of it and see the effects of its happening in my own life. The indwelling Christ is a converting presence.

In the next chapters we will look at the "stature of the fulness of Christ" into which we are being converted, and discuss how we can keep the process of conversion alive in our lives.

# 8

## *Keeping Alive the Conversion Process*

In 1966 a retrospective of Picasso's paintings was exhibited in Cannes, France. Hundreds of his works, from the first he did as an adolescent beginner to the latest of the master, who was then eighty-five years old, graced the walls of the gallery. The old man himself roamed about, enjoying the show more than anyone. One report told of a woman who stopped him and said, "I don't understand. Over there, the beginning pictures—so mature, serious and solemn—then the later ones, so different, so irrepressible. It almost seems as though the dates should be reversed. How do you explain it?"

"Easily," replied Picasso, eyes sparkling. "It takes a long time to become young."

So it does!

To be alive in Christ is constant and continuous. We are not finished, but are "under construction," maturing into the "measure of the stature of the fullness of Christ." Conversion is an ongoing process which we must keep alive. What e. e. cummings said was true for everyone has particular meaning for Christians: "We can never be born enough. We are human beings for whom birth is a supremely welcome mystery, the mystery of becoming." This is the purpose of spiritual disciplines—to keep alive the conversion process, to fertilize the seeds of potential within so that new birth and growth will happen.

Before we look at how we can keep the stage set for new births, we need to underline a subtle but significant truth. There is a difference between *following* Jesus and being *in* Christ. There is no question about the need for us to see Jesus as a model and to seek to follow him, to be *like* him, to do what he would do. Nor is there any doubt that we are *judged* by Jesus. In his presence, putting our lives alongside his, we are reminded of what is possible for our lives.

He was human. Don't forget that. But look at the new dimension he brings to our humanity. We can't look at him long and capture his spirit, and still excuse our sin and failure by claiming that we are *only* human. We look at him—and to take Christianity seriously is to really look at him—we look at him and hear his call to our *unachieved personhood*.

A Christ like that can do something for us if we let him. I look at him and I know that

He stands against my impulse to hate another who has offended me and challenges me to accept in another the defects I tolerate in myself. He stands against my indifference to the plight of others and challenges me to confirm their goodness and sustain their dignity. He stands against my desire to possess everything for myself and challenges me to share my abundance with others. He stands against my unruly love of self and challenges me to love my neighbor with the same ardor. I have given my allegiance to him because he is forever calling forth a depth and breadth of humanness in a way no one else can. (Woodyard, *Living Without God . . . Before God*)

Is this the carpenter's Son? they asked. Yes, the carpenter's Son who is human as I am human . . . not *only* human but *fully* human, calling me to my unachieved humanity.

Despite all this, the fact is that to see the patterning of lives after Jesus as the essence of Christianity misses the point. This has been the major failure of the Christian Church since the second century on. To emphasize following Jesus as the heart of Christianity is to reduce it to a religion of morals and ethics and denude it of power. This has happened over and over again in Christian history—the diminishing of the role of Jesus to merely an example for us to follow. This is one of Paul's great contributions to us; he keeps calling us back from that pitfall, reminding us, as James Stewart says,

that the example of Christ is only a part, . . . of the redeeming Gospel. Were there no more than this, the contemplation of the perfect holiness of Jesus could only breed despair. No shining example, cold and remote as the stars, can cleanse the conscience that has been defiled, or break the octopus grip which sin gets upon the soul. The evangel of an ethical example is a devastating thing. It makes religion the most grievous of burdens. Perhaps this is the real reason why, even among professing Christians, there are so many strained faces and weary hearts and captive, unreleased spirits. They have listened to Jesus' teaching, they have meditated on Jesus' character; and then they have risen up, and tried to drive their own lives along Jesus' royal way. Disappointment heaped on bitter disappointment has been the result. The great example has been a dead-weight beating them down, bearing them to the ground, bowing their hopeless souls in the dust. (*A Man in Christ*)

This is not to say that following Jesus is not important; it is simply to say that the uniqueness of the Christian faith is at another point. That point is in the experience of being in Christ, of having our lives hid with Christ in God. Jesus is not only the example we follow, he is the enabler of a new quality of life. Corrie ten Boom told how this truth came home to her. After her release from a concentration camp where her sister died, she lectured and preached all over the world about the need to forgive our enemies. She was confronted by her own message in a stunning experience. Following one of her sermons, she was greeted by a man whom she recognized as the S.S. guard at the shower room (gas chamber) at the concentration camp.

And suddenly it was all there—the roomful of mocking men, the heaps of clothing, Betsie's pain-blanched face.

He came up to me as the church was emptying, beaming and bowing. "How grateful I am for your message, *Fraulein*," he said. "To think that, as you say, He has washed my sins away!"

His hand was thrust out to shake mine. And I, who had preached so often to the people in Bloemendaal the need to forgive, kept my hand at my side.

Even as the angry, vengeful thoughts boiled through me, I saw the sin of them. Jesus Christ had died for this man; was I going to ask for more? Lord Jesus, I prayed, forgive me and help me to forgive him.

I tried to smile. I struggled to raise my hand. I could not. I felt nothing, not the slightest spark of warmth or charity. And so again I breathed a silent prayer. Jesus, I cannot forgive him. Give me Your forgiveness. As I took his hand a most incredible thing happened. From my shoulder along my arm and through my hand a current seemed to pass from me to him, while into my heart sprang a love for this stranger that almost overwhelmed me.

And so I discovered that it is not on our forgiveness any more than on our goodness that the world's healing hinges, but on His. When He tells us to love our enemies, He gives, along with the command, the love itself. *(The Hiding Place)*

The practice of forgiveness is always more difficult than the theory. Corrie ten Boom readily confessed that empowerment beyond herself worked within. Love was given by the one who told her to love her enemies.

This is more evidence for the need to cultivate awareness of the indwelling Christ.

The difference between vital Christianity, which is being alive in Christ, and Christianity as a religious system is that the latter is a dead burden we must carry, and the former is a dynamic power that carries us. Again James Stewart provides a lucid exposition of the meaning for Paul of "Christ in me."

"Christ in me" means something quite different from the weight of an impossible ideal, something far more glorious than the oppression of a pattern for ever beyond all imitation. "Christ in me" means Christ bearing me along from within, Christ the motive-power that carries me on, Christ giving my whole life a wonderful poise and lift, and turning every burden into wings. All this is in it when the apostle speaks of "Christ in you, the hope of glory" [Col. 1:27]. Compared with this, the religion which bases everything on example is pitifully rudimentary. This, and this alone, is the true Christian religion. Call it mysticism or not—the name matters little: the thing, the experience, matters, everything. To be "in Christ," to have Christ within, to realise your creed not as something you have to bear but as something by which you are borne, this is Christianity. It is more: it is release and liberty, life with an endless song at its heart. It means feeling within you, as long as life here lasts, the carrying power of Love Almighty; and underneath you, when you come to die, the touch of everlasting arms. (*A Man in Christ*)

Again it is necessary to remind ourselves of my working definition of spiritual formation and prayer. Spiritual formation is that dynamic process of receiving by faith and appropriating through commitment, discipline, and action, the living Christ into our life to the end that our life will conform to, and manifest the reality of Christ's presence in the world. Prayer and prayerful living is recognizing, cultivating awareness of, and giving expression to the indwelling Christ.

Though we have not made explicit the commitment, action, and the "giving-expression-to" dimensions of the two definitions, they have been talked about in the last three chapters and will be considered again in the next two. *Discipline, recognizing,* and *cultivating awareness* are aspects we consider now. What are the paramount disciplines that enable us to recognize and cultivate awareness of the indwelling Christ in order to keep the conversion process alive? How do we get at this process in our daily lives? Here we must travel over what for some will be familiar paths. As familiar as they may be, still they are the "road less traveled," because unfortunately most of us spend our time looking for short-cuts, rather than following the designated path.

## *Scripture*

First, *we must immerse ourselves in Scripture*. It is enriching to read books about the Bible and books based on the Bible, but there is no substitute for reading the Bible itself. I would not discount for a moment the immense value of commentaries, gifts to us from centuries of biblical scholarship. Where time and situations allow, we should avail ourselves of this rich treasure. But the Spirit is not dependent on these resources, as valuable as they are, to make God's word come alive in our lives. If we live with Scripture, immersing ourselves in its content, the Spirit will guide us into the truth and fill our lives with the power of it.

It is important to know the *content* of Scripture. Only the Bible itself provides that content, but I want to trace here what I believe is the overarching theme of that content when taken as a whole.

The Bible is the story of God's dealings with humankind, and that story repeats itself with different personalities, events, details, situations, and nuances, over and over again. God creates, chooses his people, and makes a covenant (a loving contract) with them. Persons break the covenant and suffer as a result of their unfaithfulness and folly. God continues to love, calls them to repentance, renews them in relationship and gracefully bestows salvation as a gift. God is gracious and loving—a fact we must never lose sight of.

The Old Testament revelation of God revolves around three great themes: Creation, Exodus, and Covenant. Each of these is a manifestation of God's love for us in action. In creation God expresses love by giving us life. Through the Exodus God expresses love in the form of deliverance. In the Covenant God acts out love by pledging never to abandon us, to always be our God; the fidelity of that pledge is proven a thousand times over in the face of the repeated infidelity of his people.

Words of Scripture express over and over again this love

of God. "Though the mountains move and hills shake, my love shall be immovable and never fail, and my covenant of peace shall not be shaken. So says the Lord who takes pity on you" (Isa. 54:10 NEB). When we turn to the New Testament, we find the ultimate effort of God to convey to us the reality and depth of unbounded love. In a real sense all that God had done for people had not gotten through to them clearly. Then God came to us in the person of Jesus. Many interpretations have been given of the incarnation. One very true one is to say that God sent Jesus, so that God's message of love would not be a matter of words; it would take on, in the person of Jesus, the visible, tangible form of evidence that humans crave and that could not be denied.

The works that Jesus did showed that his Father's love was real. No one was too small or insignificant or sinful to escape God's loving care and concern. As Jesus healed the sick, raised the dead, and forgave the sinner, he was saying in action, "My Father is your Father and he loves you."

What Jesus did was illumined by what he said. Especially in his parables he brought home forcefully the depth of God's love. He used the simplest human images and experiences to give clear meaning to that love. Two examples will make the point.

The people to whom Jesus spoke knew the devotion of a shepherd to his sheep, so Jesus used that image to bring home the Father's love. Jesus dared to say, "I am the good shepherd; I know my own sheep and my sheep know me . . . and I lay down my life for the sheep" (John 10:14-15 NEB). In another place he makes the image even more explicit. "If one of you has a hundred sheep and loses one of them, does he not leave the ninety-nine in the open pasture and go after the missing one until he has found it? How delighted he is then! He lifts it on his shoulders, and home he goes to call his friends and neighbours together. 'Rejoice with me!' he cries, 'I have found my lost sheep'" (Luke 15:4-6 NEB). Lest the image be so simple that his learners would delight only in the story, he makes the explicit application: "I tell you, there will be more joy in heaven over one sinner who repents than over ninety-nine righteous persons who need no repentance" (Luke 15:7).

No parable of Jesus speaks of the Father's love so vividly as in the parable of the prodigal son. We all know this parable almost by heart, but we need to read and ponder it time and time again. Almost every time we read and pray over it, we will see something new in it. It touches all the elements of the human experience of sin; the impetuosity and shortsightedness with which the son requested his share of the inheritance; the haste with which he squandered everything with no thought of the consequences; the sudden awareness of what he had done; the feeling of unworthiness that prevented him even considering that his father might still love him. From the sheer motive of survival, the son decides to return home. He very carefully prepares a speech. In that speech he never even considers the possibility of anything but rejection by his father. The real grandeur of the parable is revealed when he actually does return. Jesus is very explicit in saying that "When the son was still a long way off, the father saw him." In other words, the father was waiting all along for his son's return; he has never ceased to love this wayward son and hope for his return. He goes out to meet his son and embraces him. When the son tries to make his carefully prepared speech, he is interrupted. His Father is not interested in it. A celebration is called for by the simple reason that "This son of mine was dead and has come back to life. He was lost and is found." (Cf. Luke 15:11-30)

This is every person's parable. Pondering it, who can question or doubt what God's attitude toward us is? God loves us with an unbounded, undying love. Isaiah provides a beautiful image of it, as he records God speaking: "Can a woman forget the infant at her breast, or a loving mother the child of her womb? Even these forget, yet I will not forget you" (Isa. 49:15 NEB).

As we immerse ourselves in Scripture, familiarizing ourselves with its content, all sorts of conversions will take place. We can begin with a passage which has special meaning for us and which we especially need. I have a friend who has been reading the Book of Proverbs once each month for five years. She says she needs the practical wisdom it provides. My friend Tom Carruth has read I John every day for twenty years. Is it any wonder that he is such a vibrant witness of love?

It is important that we deliberately live not only with sections of Scripture that address our particular needs, but also with those that confront and challenge—calling us to conversion. No Christian should go long without rereading the Sermon on the Mount which is Jesus' manifesto of the kingdom. When we find ourselves too much "at home" with our world, too comfortable and secure with our social and political systems, we need to go back to the prophets, especially Isaiah, Amos, and Micah. When we are experiencing dryness in our spiritual journey, we need to baptize ourselves in the Psalms and experience the ups-and-downs of those who gave intimate testimony to their relationship with God. When we grow weary in the church, and forget that we are seeking to be God's people, we need to turn to Paul's letters to the young churches, and get our bearing again.

It is not enough to know the content of Scripture; that tends to be only a "head trip." We must open ourselves to the Scripture, so that the Spirit may work with converting power within us. We will consider one way of doing this as we talk now about a second discipline which opens us to an expanding awareness of the indwelling Christ—the discipline of *prayer*.

## Prayer of Imagination and Memory

I have written two books on prayer, *The Workbook of Living Prayer* and *The Workbook of Intercessory Prayer*. These are practical, experiential manuals on learning to pray, but they are incomplete as all books on prayer are, because we never become "masters of prayer." There is always *more*, more to learn, more to experience, more to receive. Therefore when I say that *prayer is recognizing, cultivating awareness of, and*

*giving expression to the indwelling Christ,* I am not contending
that that is all prayer is. I am simply saying that this is a
working understanding and practice that provides growth
and meaning as I seek to be alive in Christ.

Considering this focused aspect of prayer, I want to suggest
a way of praying which is related to immersing ourselves in
Scripture. This form of prayer has been developed in many
ways and is variously called "imagery meditation," "prayer
of Christ's memories," "prayer of personal reminiscence,"
"imagination journeys with Christ," and other names. The
*Ignatian Exercises* are rooted in this form of prayer. Archie
Matson in *A Month with the Master* (a book now out of print)
sought to make the Ignatian system more contemporary. The
pattern I offer here is drawn from all these various
expressions, with a focus on cultivating awareness of, and
responding to the indwelling Christ. I am specifically
dependent on a Jesuit priest, David J. Hassel, for bringing this
into a particular shape for my own practice. He calls it "prayer
of Christ's memories."

The pattern is a simple one. First, select a passage from
the Gospels. It is best at the beginning to use stories of Jesus'
activity and ministry (not his sermons or parables)—i.e., his
healing of the blind man (John 9:1-25), the party at Simon's
house when the woman of the street anointed his feet (Luke
7:36-50), the woman caught in adultery and brought before
Jesus for stoning (John 8:1-11), the storm on the Sea of
Galilee stilled by Jesus (Mark 4:35-41).

Second, read the passage slowly, aloud if circumstances
permit. Having read the story, close your eyes for thirty
seconds or so, and get the scene in your imagination. Do a
second oral reading, noticing details you missed in the first
reading. Again close your eyes for thirty seconds or so,
allowing these new details to fit into the total scene in your
imagination. A third reading will give even more details.
Questions and insights will begin to rise as you close your
eyes in silence to let your imagination work. In a fourth or
maybe a fifth leisurely reading, distractions will disappear

and your imagination will be saturated by this Gospel scene.

Third, now simply close your Bible and your eyes. Let the scene happen in your imagination. Do not try to make something happen, just stay alert to whatever developments take place.

Fourth, as you settle into the Gospel episode—e.g., the party at Simon's house that is "crashed" by the woman of ill-repute—you will tend to lose sense of yourself and to identify with the situation: a festive party, tables laden with delicious food, jovial conversation, people talking to one another, some listening to Jesus and Simon. If the identification deepens—and it does the more you practice this pattern—you will find yourself at the party, e.g., as a person eating and conversing. Then, as further identification occurs, you may find yourself as Simon, or the woman, or even Christ. It is not unusual to find yourself drifting in and out of the scene, in and out of various people.

Fifth, it is important to note that you are not substituting or displacing Simon, or the woman, or Jesus in the story. Rather, you are entering into their feelings, hopes, thoughts, or actions. There are other types of prayer when you may want to seek in your imagination to be the other persons. But in this kind of praying you are seeking to be as passive as possible, so there should be no subjective "forcing of yourself" into the scene. Be alert, listening, watching—conversing with the Gospel situation, but not argumentative.

You may find this type prayer very difficult when you first begin to practice it. Most of us are so used to controlling every situation that it is difficult to break the pattern, even in our praying. Here you are letting the persons in the story control or guide; above all you are risking yieldedness to the Gospel, the event of the Gospel and to Christ in the Gospel, so that you forget yourself and the Spirit takes over, using your imagination to bring alive the Gospel and its unique message for your life.

Sixth, you will seriously hamper, even nullify altogether, the meaning and power of this kind of praying if you seek to moralize, or make clever applications, or draw theological conclusions. To do any of these brings the focus back to you—which may be appropriate in other types of praying, but not here. The secret of this prayer of Christ's memories is to lose oneself in the Gospel situation and its people. To pray in this fashion is to trust that the Gospel events live now in the dynamic memory of the risen Christ, and to identify ourselves selflessly with these memories of his which are the living Word. In this kind of praying we are trusting the Spirit of the risen Christ, who is the same Christ who sat with Simon at the dinner, received the worship of the woman, confronted Simon with his sin, and affirmed to the woman and all who came after her that "the one who is forgiven much loves much."

Seventh, when you feel you have finished your absorption in this gospel event, move on to another, and repeat the process. Sometimes you will involve yourself in two or three scenes in one period, sometimes only one. It is helpful to move through one Gospel to absorb the content of it. Also again in this fashion you are not in control; you are taking the events as they come and letting them be for you what they will be by the work of the Spirit. I would suggest the Gospel of Mark as a beginning because it is so energy-packed and fast-moving.

This type of prayer may be adapted in many ways, but I urge that the pattern suggested here be followed precisely without alteration until the dynamic begins to work in your experience. Once you are convinced of the effectiveness of it and are comfortable with the style, you can practice variations on the theme.

I do not want to suggest that this kind of prayer become your whole prayer life. Nor am I suggesting it as a daily exercise, though in the beginning you may wish to make it so. It does take about thirty minutes to give sufficient attention to the process, especially in the beginning.

## *Being Quiet Before the Word*

One very practical variation on this theme that is quite easy to effect in your daily life involves more active reflection on your part. It is what I call "being quiet before the Word." This pattern is not so passive and calls for the use of imagination and reflection. The outline of the process is as follows:

1. Center down, deliberately placing yourself in the presence of God.

2. Be quiet before the Word. Select a passage of Scripture (the parables of Jesus especially lend themselves to this approach). Read the passage slowly, giving it your full attention.

3. Be passively open. Don't try to "figure things out," but be open to leading and suggestion. Don't try to impose your rationalization or logic on the Scripture at this point.

4. Deliberately focus your mind on the Scripture. Let your imagination become active, cooperating with God in becoming aware of whatever thoughts or feelings come from the content of the Scripture you are considering. This cooperation may take many forms. Honest struggling and searching are signs of your willingness and sincerity to hear God's Word addressed to you. When you do find yourself struggling over a tough or obscure saying, make sure it's a cooperative struggling!

5. Listen to the Scripture speaking to you. What would you feel if you were one or another of the persons in the Scripture? Try to get in touch with your own feelings as you respond to the action or relationships or attitudes present in the Scripture with which you are living.

6. Make whatever application to your life that seems appropriate. Deal with the feelings that come.

In this final step in the process you are actively reflecting.

Reflecting is different from purer forms of meditation in which you seek not to reflect but simply *receive* what comes.

## Contemplation and Action

Immersing ourselves in Scripture, and prayer that focuses on cultivating an awareness of the indwelling Christ lead to a form of spirituality that deserves a lot of attention—that is, to action. Solitude and solidarity are so inseparably linked that the contemplative life is not a life separated from the world; it is intimately involved in the world, and acts—many times at great cost—as Christ in the world. "Giving expression to the indwelling Christ" is a vital part of my working understanding of prayer; the phrase "manifest the reality of Christ's presence in the world" is integral to my definition of spiritual formation.

There is a real sense in which prayer is political activity. Contemplative prayer and social criticism are connected. Thomas Merton, the Trappist monk from the Abbey of Gethsemane in Kentucky who died in 1968, has shown this connection dramatically in recent times. Daniel Berrigan was reflecting this connection when he said, "The time will shortly be upon us, if it is not already here, when the pursuit of contemplation becomes a strictly subversive activity."

The point is that solitude and interior prayer, cultivating an awareness of the indwelling Christ, is very closely linked with the awakening of the social conscience. In solitude, alone with ourselves and God, our awareness of the indwelling Christ is quickened and we are given perception and vision. Our awareness of the world's needs is intensified, our perception of ourselves as participants in systems that promulgate suffering, poverty, and oppression is sharpened, we become aware of our sin and are driven to repent. We also stand back contemplatively and see things as Christ sees them. Then we have a vision that motivates and determines the forms and direction of our action. Kenneth Leech has given us a good perspective:

It is wrong to stress the virtues of compassion, love and sensitivity to people in Christ, and to ignore the New Testament's frequent warnings against blindness and lack of perception. It is more important to see clearly than to behave well, for action arises from vision. The contemplative who can stand back from a situation and see it for what it is is more threatening to an unjust social system than the frenzied activist who is so involved in the situation that he cannot see clearly at all.

I remember vividly a conversation I had with Anthony Bloom, the Russian Orthodox who has written so helpfully in the area of prayer (*Living Prayer*, *School of Prayer*, and *Courage to Pray*, all published by Darton, Longman & Todd, London). We were filming the conversation to use as a resource for teaching, especially in prayer groups, schools of prayer, and retreats. At one point we were talking about the connection between contemplation and action, and I asked Metropolitan Bloom to define contemplation. He responded.

Well I think this is where contemplation begins. Sit and listen—in religious terms it may be called waiting on God—but it's simply plain listening or looking in order to hear and to understand. If we did that with regard to the Word of God, with regard to the prayers of the saints, with regard to the situations in which we are, to everything people say to us or what they are in life, with regard to our own selves—we would be in that condition which one can call contemplation, which consists in pondering, thinking deeply, in waiting until one has understood in order to act. Then action would be much more efficient, less hasty, and filled, probably, with some amount of the Divine Wisdom.

That is a clear definition, but he made it even clearer by using two images. One was a nursery rhyme he learned in the United States.

A Wise old owl
lived in an oak;
The more he saw
the less he spoke.
The less he spoke,
the more he heard.

Why can't we all be
like that bird?

His second image he borrowed from the English mystic
and writer Evelyn Underhill. A Christian should be like a
sheep dog. When the shepherd wants the dog to do
something, the dog lies down at his master's feet, looks
intently into the shepherd's eyes, and listens without
budging until he has understood the mind of the master.
Then he jumps to his feet and runs to do it. And, equally
important, at no moment does the dog stop wagging its tail.

It is that sort of understanding that enables Bloom to write
so simply and clearly, to apply the most profound truths
about prayer and spirituality to our practical everyday
situation. In his book *Courage to Pray* he illumines
intercession and the connection between contemplation
and action by talking about the role of Mary in Jesus' first
miracle—the turning of water to wine in Cana (John 2:1-11).
The story is confusing in many ways, especially in the
disjointed conversation between Jesus and Mary. Mary told
him that the hosts had run out of wine. In what mood Jesus
responds we do not know, but his words are baffling,
maybe even a rebuke: "Is that your concern or mine? What
have you to do with me? My hour has not yet come." What
grace Mary shows! She doesn't challenge Jesus, or question
his kindness and compassion to her. She simply tells the
servants to do whatever Jesus tells them.

Bloom says that instead of answering Jesus, Mary "brings
the kingdom by showing she has perfect faith in him, that
the words she has pondered in her heart from the beginning
have been fruitful and she sees him for what he is, the word
of God." Then Bloom makes an adroit and concrete
application.

We too can be in the same situation as Mary. We too can make
God's kingdom come, wherever we are, in spite of the unbelief of
the people we are with. Simply by having complete faith in the
Lord and thus showing ourselves to be children of the kingdom.

This is a crucially important act of intercession. The fact that we are present in a situation alters it profoundly because God is then present with us through our faith. Wherever we are, at home with our family, with friends when a quarrel is about to begin, at work or even simply in the underground, the street, the train, we can recollect ourselves and say, 'Lord I believe in you, come and be among us.' And by this act of faith, in a contemplative prayer which does not ask to see, we can intercede with God who has promised his presence when we ask for it. Sometimes we have no words, sometimes we do not know how to act wisely, but we can always ask God to come and be present. And we shall see how often the atmosphere changes, quarrels stop, peace comes. This is not a minor mode of intercession, although it is less spectacular than a great sacrifice. We see in it again how contemplation and action are inseparable, that Christian action is impossible without contemplation. We see also how such contemplation is not a vision of God alone, but a deep vision of everything enabling us to see its eternal meaning. Contemplation is a vision not of God alone, but of the world in God. *(Courage to Pray)*

We keep the process of conversion alive by this sort of contemplative living.

## *Christian Community*

The conversion process is also kept alive by Christian community. *Community* is the core of the Christian life. *Koinonia* was the Greek word used for it. We translate the word as "fellowship" but that is far too weak.

What is abundantly clear both from the New Testament and from the writings of the early fathers is the fact that the early Christians saw themselves as part of a new creation, the 'age to come,' whose powers were already at work. They were shaping a new pattern for the human community, a pattern of love and sharing, the pattern of the social life of God himself. 'Your Kingdom come, your will be done, *on earth as in heaven*' meant, literally, that the life-style of the Godhead was to be manifested within the human community. A contemporary Indian Christian, Samuel Rayan, has expressed it thus: 'New Testament spirituality is the spirituality of broken bread (our earth) and shared wine (a life of friendship).'

The Christian community thus witnesses to the life of the

Kingdom, the life of God, not only in its preaching, but in its life. But this involves suffering, for *koinonia* in Christ is a sharing in his cross (Phil. 3:8-10). Our prayer is Kingdom-centred because it is oriented towards the coming of the 'age to come,' on earth as in heaven. All prayer is social, because it is rooted in *koinonia*, sharing, in the life of God. And all prayer is therefore political, because it is an essential element in the transformation of the world.

One aspect of Christian community is absolutely essential, though it is most often forgotten, and when kept alive can make the Christian community the place and the dynamic for the shaping power of the indwelling Christ to be most dramatically alive. That aspect is *mutual submission*. It may well be that the reason efforts at Christian community often fail, and what goes under the banner "Church" is only a pale reflection of the real thing, is that the spiritual discipline of submission is not practiced within our fellowship. That may also be the reason our fellowship stops short of being true *koinonia*.

Martin Luther put the discipline of submission in perspective. "A Christian man is the most free lord of all, and subject to none; a Christian man is the most dutiful servant of all, and subject to everyone." Luther understood the clearest and most meaningful expression of the biblical meaning of submission given by Jesus himself: "Anyone who wishes to be a follower of mine must leave self behind; he must take up his cross, and come with me. Whoever cares for his own safety is lost; but if a man will let himself be lost for my sake and for the Gospel, that man is safe" (Mark 8:34-35 NEB).

Paul stated this truth in a straightforward way: "Be subject to one another out of reverence for Christ" (Eph. 5:21; Phil. 2:3). This is a call to all Christians to have an attitude of mutual submission and service to one another.

We cower at this hard word of Jesus and Paul's elaboration of it. Self-fulfillment and self-actualization speak softly and gently to our ears. Self-denial cuts to the quick of our feeling and challenges us at the core of our being. No one need remind us that we are self-seeking, self-serving, self-indulging people. Yet this is something we have not wanted to talk about. A blatant emphasis on self-seeking and self-serving has flowered in the sixties and the seventies. This may be one of the most telling signs of our decadence. A spate of books on such themes as self-assertion and "winning through intimidation" have touted a philosophy of getting ahead and exercising personal power for selfish gain. This is a perversion of self-actualization or self-fulfillment. Jesus knew, and Paul was echoing the truth, that self-fulfillment involves self-denial. But self-denial does not mean self-hatred or self-mortification. It does not mean the rejection of our individuality. Self-denial is a way by which we realize that our happiness and fulfillment are not dependent upon having our own way or getting what we want. Self-denial is the willingness to consider the needs of others above our own self-interest. It is a commitment to live in relationships where the worth of all persons are valued and where "getting my own way" gives way to considering the concerns, needs, and interests of others.

Self-actualization or self-fulfillment is not the opposite of self-denial. Self-denial, according to Jesus, is the only road to self-fulfillment. We save our lives by losing them for Christ's sake. Willingness to be last makes us "first." Again, it must be made clear if we are to have a creative, redemptive understanding of submission, that self-denial is not the same thing as self-contempt.

Unfortunately, some expressions of Christian piety have equated the two. To a marked degree, as already indicated, the monastic movement was a world-denying, self-mortification movement that stimulated an ascetic spirituality in which the flesh was evil and had to be "whipped" into subjection to the Spirit. This was rooted in a misunderstanding of Paul's teaching about "flesh and spirit" and denied God's affirmation of his creation as *good*. Thus, self-denial issued in self-contempt. To practice self-denial out of a stance of self-contempt never produces the abundant life of joy which is the birthright of persons *in Christ*.

Jesus made the ability to love ourselves the foundation for loving and reaching out to others (Matt. 22:39). Self-contempt says we have no worth; self-denial declares that we are of infinite worth, as are others, and that life is found in the rhythm of affirming ourselves and others as we love others as ourselves. It is in this context that submission is to be understood and practiced.

Submission is an ethical theme that runs throughout the New Testament. It is to be the posture of all Christians because we are to follow the crucified Lord who emptied himself to become the servant of all. Submission is the cross-style to which we are called. Jesus not only died a cross-death, he lived a cross-life of submission and service. We will consider this more in chapter 10.

Though speaking about another matter, Thomas A. Langford gives a seldom thought of meaning to the koinonia of mutual submission.

Our strength, as Christians, comes from our relation to God and to the people of God. We are directly related to God, and in that relationship we find our ability to move to action and to live for others. Indirectly we receive the strength of God through sharing in Christian community. This is a sharing which empowers, guides, corrects, and renews our ability to be and to serve.

Emphasis upon Christian strength is often neglected for fear of abuse, and the strength given by community is often neglected because it is so meagerly realized in contemporary experience. Yet the church is the Body of Christ; it is the special embodiment of the Holy Spirit. The church is the community graciously given by God to persons who need and who intensely seek community. Into our solitary, isolated style of living there comes a concrete community of persons who are willing to bear one another's burdens, to enhance one another's living, to be together in joy and in sorrow, in hope and in hurt, at ordinary moments and in critical junctures of human experience.

In the context of the church, strength comes from lives which are bound together. The chief binding is not that of a desperate clinging to one another in a dangerous and frightening world. . . . The deeper truth, however, is that persons in Christian community are bound together by a common love, by a common worship, and by a common mission. The church is the community of persons who are in community with Jesus Christ. It is a community of persons precisely because there is a common center for their lives. *(Christian Wholeness)*

The center Langford speaks of is Christ. When the indwelling Christ is the shaping power of the people in the community, they can give themselves to one another in love and mutual submission. I doubt if there is a more radical call to conversion than this, and I doubt if there is anything that could transform the lives of Christians more than to begin the practice of being "subject to one another out of reverence for Christ" (Eph. 5:21).

## Spiritual Friendship

*Spiritual friendship* is another practice that keeps alive the conversion process. This is Christian community distilled to its concentrated essence. Spiritual friendship may find expression in small groups, sometimes called "koinonia groups." These are designed to be a setting where a few people can find a place to *belong*, where warmth of acceptance, love, nonjudgmental listening, honest sharing, and prayer can be experienced personally and intimately. In my nearly thirty years as a minister I have seen more dramatic and permanent changes in persons take place in small group settings such as this than any place else.

Bob was part of a sharing group of men who ate breakfast, talked, and prayed together every Friday morning in the church I served in Anaheim, California. He wasn't with us long before we knew something was wrong. He was unable to share. When the discussion seemed to come close to him, he would back away and shut himself off from conversation. Or he would do the opposite—hide behind a lot of meaningless talk. Then he left the group. I had known for some time, and the other men soon discovered, that he and his wife were having problems. The other men did not know, as I did, that he was really leading a double life. He was living with another woman other than his wife, walking roughshod over his wife's feelings, pledging integrity but sustaining it only for a short period, then falling back into duplicity and shame.

Bob was away from the church and the sharing group for three months. When he returned, he confessed that the strength to return—to face his wife and children, to seek forgiveness and build a new life—came in the knowledge that in that fellowship of sharing he would be accepted and would find the support for painstakingly rebuilding all that he had shattered. He knew the support would not be a Pollyanna acceptance, or a hiding from truth, or a veiling of sin and judgment. His shame and guilt would not be ignored, but in that group he would find the practice Paul called for: "If a man should do something wrong . . . you who are endowed with the Spirit must set him right again very gently. Look to yourself, each one of you: you may be tempted too. Help one another to carry these heavy loads, and in this way you will fulfil the law of Christ" (Gal. 6:1-2 NEB).

Even in a more particularized setting than the small group, spiritual friendship may be practiced in a one-to-one relationship. This may be a relationship in which two people are drawn together out of mutual need and respect, or it may be a deliberate relationship that is formalized by a covenant. Feeling a deep need for spiritual guidance and/or counseling, one person may seek another whom she trusts and to whom she is willing to risk herself in sharing and receiving what guidance the other person offers. In the history of the church there is the tradition of "Spiritual Directors" or "Spiritual Guides." This is a ministry that we need to recover. Tilden Edwards and Kenneth Leech have written helpful books in this field (*Spiritual Friend,* published by Paulist Press, and *Soul Friend*, published by Sheldon Press, London). Any Christian community will be well served to study these two books and emphasize this particular ministry.

Though it is meaningful to see "spiritual" or "soul" friendship in a somewhat specialized way, I believe that all Christians are called, and to a marked degree gifted, to be and to have a spiritual friend. While perhaps the greatest possibility for change can come in a sustained relationship of love and sharing, I believe that even brief encounters can be occasions for Christ to be so powerfully present that we will be changed. The key is our believing that Christ is alive and working in the people we meet, and that his Spirit is transferrable—that in relationships where he is acknowledged he can and will do his transforming work.

I have deliberately not dealt with corporate worship and the sacraments in this chapter. If I were writing an entire book on spiritual disciplines and ways to keep the conversion process alive, these would probably top the list. I have simply wanted to underscore here the reality of the need, and indicate some perhaps neglected or little-thought-of-ways that we can recognize, cultivate awareness of, and give expression to the indwelling Christ as a source of continuing conversion. The following chapters will emphasize the *expressing* aspect of our being alive in Christ.

# 9

## *Being Christ*

Malcolm Muggeridge closed his biography of Mother Teresa of Calcutta with this word:

It will be for posterity to decide whether she is a saint. I only say of her that in a dark time she is a burning and a shining light; in a cruel time, a living embodiment of Christ's gospel of love; in a godless time, the Word dwelling among us, full of grace and truth. *(Something Beautiful for God)*

I assume Muggeridge is using the word *saint* in a specialized way. For me I see no need to leave the question for posterity. The Christian saint is a Christian individual in full degree. That is the end toward which we all move—*to be Christian in full degree,* and that means to be alive in Christ. Jacopone da Todi put it clearly: a saint is "one in whom Christ is felt to live again." Mother Teresa would not claim it, but her life is a transparent witness of it, and her words have the ring of authenticity because of who she is and what she does. Hear her.

Because we cannot see Christ we cannot express our love to him; but our neighbours we can always see, and we can do to them what if we saw him we would like to do to Christ. . . .

It is a danger; if we forget to whom we are doing it. Our works are only an expression of our love for Christ. Our hearts need to be full of love for him and since we have to express that love in action, naturally then the poorest of the poor are the means of expressing our love for God. . . .

Because it is a continual contact with Christ in his work, it is the same contact we have during Mass and in the Blessed Sacrament. There we have Jesus in the appearance of bread. But here in the slums, in the broken body, in the children, we see Christ and we touch him. *(Something Beautiful for God)*

Again, my working understanding of prayer and spiritual formation requires the presence of the Incarnation of God in Jesus Christ to become a personal reality in us. Our prayer and our life is in Christ. Being spiritually formed as Christians means being conformed to Christ's life, *so that our lives manifest the reality of his presence in the world.* Prayer and prayerful living is recognizing and cultivating the awareness of Christ's presence and expressing that presence in our relationships in the world. As we grow vividly alive in Christ, his Spirit is expressed through us, and the fantastic and thrilling rubric for our lives becomes a viable possibility: *we will be Christ to, and/or receive Christ from every person we meet.*

We focus now on *being Christ to others.* What Christ has been and done for us we must do and be for others. Our life in Christ and our ministry in his name are inseparable. A spirituality that does not lead to active ministry becomes an indulgent preoccupation with self, and therefore grieves the Holy Spirit and violates the presence of the indwelling Christ.

Paul's powerful prayer in Ephesians is a profound expression of our call to live a life in Christ, and an amazing affirmation of God's power working in us to fulfill that ministry. "I pray that the God of our Lord Jesus Christ, the all-glorious Father, may give you the spiritual powers of wisdom and vision, by which there comes the knowledge of him. I pray that your inward eyes may be illumined, so that you may know what is the hope to which he calls you, what the wealth and glory of the share he offers you among his people in their heritage, and how vast the resources of his power open to us who trust in him. They are measured by his strength and might which he exerted in Christ when he raised him from the dead" (vv. 17-20 NEB).

The "share he offers" is our share in the life of Christ which is the heritage of all Christians. Paul talks about this especially in terms of our sharing in the resurrection of Christ. Commenting on this prayer, Henri Nouwen says,

This prayer makes clear that the spiritual life is a life guided by the same Spirit who guided Jesus Christ. The Spirit is the breath of Christ in us, the divine power of Christ active in us, the mysterious source of new vitality by which we are made aware that it is not we who live, but Christ who lives in us. . . . Indeed, to live a spiritual life means to become living Christs. It is not enough to try to imitate Christ as much as possible; it is not enough to remind others of Jesus; it is not even enough to be inspired by the words and actions of Jesus Christ. No, the spiritual life presents us with a far more radical demand: to be living Christs here and now, in time and history. (*Sojourners*, June 1981)

Radical? Yes. And more radical yet when we realize that this is not a call to some "special vocation"; this is the call to every person who would be Christian. The Christian life is life as Jesus lived it and now lives it in us.

Lest some seek to sidetrack the powerful thrust of this challenge, contending that this message about being in Christ and living Christ's life in the world comes from Paul and not from Jesus himself, we need to ponder Jesus' own message. In his metaphor of the vine and branches Jesus calls us to *abide* in him, and allow him to abide in us. His prayer in the Upper Room when he celebrated the last Passover with his disciples is full of his longing, his deep yearning for all his followers.

It is not for these alone that I pray [his disciples], but for those also who through their words put their faith in me; may they all be one:

as thou, Father, art in me, and I in thee, *so also may they be in us*, that the world may believe that thou didst send me. The glory which thou gavest me I have given to them, that they may be one, as we are one; *I in them* and thou in me, may they be perfectly one. Then the world will learn that thou didst send me, that thou didst love them as thou didst me. . . .

I made thy name known to them, and will make it known, so that the love thou hadst for me may be in them, and *I may be in them."* (John 17:20-26 NEB, italics mine)

Not only does Jesus call us to abide in him, to be one with him and the Father, he makes it scathingly clear that he is in others and the way we treat others will be the measure of our judgment. "As you did it to one of the least of these my brethren, you did it to me" (Matt. 25:40). So we cannot be sidetracked from the call. It came originally from Jesus who even insisted that we would do greater things than he because he was going to the Father, and would return to abide in Spirit with us, filling us with power, giving us wisdom and insight, comfort and companionship, and guiding us to truth. Paul responded to Jesus' call, worked the call out in his own life—"it is not I, but Christ lives in me"—and shared the vision with us.

Carlo Carretto gives a powerful and challenging witness of this truth coming home to him. At the age of forty-four, after a life of intense social involvement with Catholic Action in Italy during the turbulent years following World War Two, he felt the call to the desert. Driven by this call, he left Italy for North Africa, where he joined the Little Brothers of Jesus without knowing anything of their rules, and embraced the way of life of Charles de Foucauld, the founder of the order, of whom he had not previously heard.

The desert has always been looked upon as an anvil on which the human spirit can be shaped. Carretto was mysteriously drawn to the Sahara, unconsciously knowing that the immensity of the desert would overwhelm both his power and his weakness; and there in the vast emptiness of the trackless sand, he would be able to experience the vast emptiness and uselessness of his own soul, and find that undiluted communion with God for which he starvingly yearned.

Early in his desert sojourn, he had an experience that shaped his life. He was resting, in midday, beneath the welcome shade of some huge rocks, taking the traditional desert siesta before his meal. To tell his story in my words would diminish the power of it. So, here it is, in his words.

In order to lie more comfortably I looked for a blanket to put under my head. I had two. One remained by my side unused, and as I looked at it I could not feel at ease.

But to understand you must hear my story.

The evening before I had passed through Irafog, a small village of Negroes, ex-slaves of the Tuareg. As usual when one reaches a village the people ran out to crowd around the jeep, either from curiosity, or to obtain the various things which desert-travellers bring with them: they may bring a little tea, distribute medicines or hand over letters.

That evening I had seen old Kada trembling with cold. It seems strange to speak of cold in the desert, but it is so; in fact the Sahara is often called "a cold country where it is very hot in the sun." The sun had gone down, and Kada was shivering. I had the idea of giving him one of the blankets I had with me, an essential part of my *ghess*; but I put the thought out of my mind. I thought of the night and I knew that I, too, would shiver. The little charity that was in me made me think again, though reasoning that my skin wasn't worth more than his and that I had best give him one of the blankets. Even if I shivered a little that was the least a Little Brother could do.

When I left the village the blankets were still on the jeep; and now they were giving me a bad conscience.

I tried to get to sleep with my feet resting on the great rock, but I couldn't manage it. I remembered that a month ago a Tuareg in the middle of his siesta had been crushed by a falling slab. I got up to make sure how stable the boulder was; I saw that it was a little off-balance, but not enough to be dangerous.

I lay down again on the sand. If I were to tell you what I dreamed of you would find it strange. The funny thing is that I dreamed that I was asleep under the great boulder and that at a given moment—it didn't seem to be a dream at all: I saw the rock moving, and I felt the boulder fall on top of me. What a nightmare!

I felt my bones grating and I found myself dead. No, alive, but with my body crushed under the stone. I was amazed that not a bone hurt; but I could not move. I opened my eyes and saw Kada shivering in front of me at Irafog. I didn't hesitate for a minute to give him the blanket, especially as it was lying unused behind me, a yard away. I tried to stretch out my hand to offer it to him; but the stone made even the smallest movement impossible. I understood what purgatory was and that the suffering of the soul was "no longer to have the possibility of doing what before one could and should have done." Who knows for how many years afterwards I would be haunted by seeing that blanket near me as a witness to my selfishness and to the fact that I was too immature to enter the Kingdom of Love.

I tried to think of how long I was to remain under the rock. The reply was given me by the catechism: "Until you are capable of an act of perfect love." At that moment I felt quite incapable.

The perfect act of love is Jesus going up to Calvary to die for us all. As a member of his Mystical Body I was being asked to show if I was close enough to that perfect love to follow my master to Calvary for the salvation of my brethren. The presence of the blanket denied to Kada the evening before told me that I had still a long way to go. If I were capable of passing by a brother who was shivering with cold, how should I be capable of dying for him in imitation of Jesus who died for us all? In this way I understood that I was lost, and that if somebody had not come to my aid, I should have lain there, aeon after aeon, without being able to move.

I looked away and realised that all those great rocks in the desert were nothing more than the tombs of other men. They too, judged according to their ability to love and found cold, were there to await him who once said, "I shall raise you up on the last day." *(Letters from the Desert)*

It is a dramatic story. The Sahara is far, far away. The vocation of a Little Brother of Jesus is something most of us cannot even begin to understand. Yet, Caretto's story is a parable at least of the call and the possibility that is offered each of us: to be Christ to and/or receive Christ from every person we meet. With no claims to anything new, and certainly with no thought of offering a complete picture of what it means to be a living Christ here and now in our time and place, I want to discuss two areas of concern which I believe clamor for attention. Then in the last chapter I will suggest two elements which I believe are pivotal in developing a Christ style which will manifest his presence in all the world.

## *Affirming Presence*

As the indwelling Christ is an affirming presence in our lives, so we must be his affirming presence to others.

In the first chapter of his Gospel, with almost breathtaking succinctness and rapidity, Mark tells the story of Jesus' forty days in the wilderness, his call and baptism, then his call of the disciples, and his beginning ministry in a series of healings. One of those healings was of a leper (Mark 1:40-45). In New Testament times, leprosy was the most dreaded of all diseases. The victim not only suffered physical debilitation, but also mental and emotional pain and anguish. Lepers were forced to live alone; they had to wear special clothing so others could identify them and avoid them. Perhaps the most abysmal humiliation was that they were required by law to announce vocally their despicable condition: *Unclean! Unclean!*

Mark tells of one of these lepers coming boldly to Jesus, kneeling before him and appealing, "If you want to, you can make me clean." Then there is packed into one beautiful sentence almost everything Jesus was and was about. "Jesus was filled with pity for him, and stretched out his hand and placed it on the leper, saying, 'Of course I want to—*be clean!*'" (Mark 1:41 Phillips). That tells it all! Stay with that encounter for a moment to get the full impact of it. By law the leper had no right to even draw near Jesus, much less speak to him. How, we do not know, but he knew that despite his repulsive disease, his grotesque appearance, Jesus would *see him*, really see him, and respond to him as a person, not as a maimed, disfigured piece of flesh. Note Jesus' response: he *listened*, he *looked* at him, and he *touched* him—the three action-responses that no one else would dare make.

I could have chosen more stories—Zacchaeus, the woman at the well, or others—that make the same point. But I deliberately share this one to make the point more graphically. If Jesus' ministry goes to the point of involving him with the poorest of the poor, the ugliest of the ugly, can there be any question that we must move through our days responding in affirming love and care to the persons whose lives intersect ours?

Jesus *listened* to the leper. Is there anything that enhances our feelings of worth more than being listened to? When you listen to me you say to me, "I value you. You are important. I will hear what you say."

Jesus *looked* at him. He gave the leper his attention. When we listen and look at another, we are *attending*. Someone has defined *thought* as "man in his fullness fully attending." That is more than thought, it is affirming relationship: a person in his fullness fully attending another person. That sort of attending is the context in which the Spirit comes alive in relationship. It is a listening with mind and heart out of which comes revelation. When I listen in this fashion, the gap between the other person and me is bridged. A sensitivity comes that is not my own. I feel the pain, frustration, and anguish. Healing, reconciliation, strength, guidance are the miracles of love that take place when I attend, when I listen and look in the spirit of the indwelling Christ.

Jesus *touched* the leper. To be an affirming presence in the style of the indwelling Christ, we must touch. We cannot remain aloof; we must deliberately reach out, touch, and become involved. In his book *On Being Human*, G. Marian Kinget discusses the illuminating and piercing points made by Fritz Perls and later by Walter Tubbs that while in our day love is doing very well academically, as evidenced by the growing amount of literature on the subject, existentially and experientially love is in short supply, even in a state of crisis.

Something of the essence of the contemporary love crisis and of its possible remedy seems to be contained in the following poem. The first part, the widely known lines by Fritz Perls, contains much that is true and practical—though severely limited. It offers a *modus vivendi* for individuals living *among* other individuals, not *with* them. In other words, it does not offer a model for a relationship, for it leaves out the warmth, the care and concern that form the essence of human commerce. The second part, by Tubbs, beautifully supplements the first by stressing the need for awareness and mindfulness of the other, and for active reaching out for mutuality.

### BEYOND PERLS†

*I do my thing, and you do your thing.*
*I am not in this world to live up to your expectations,*
*And you are not in this world to live up to mine.*
*You are you and I am I;*
*If by chance we find each other, it's beautiful.*
*If not, it can't be helped.†† (Fritz Perls)*

If I just do my thing and you do yours,
We stand in danger of losing each other
And ourselves.

I am not in this world to live up to your expectations;
But I am in this world to confirm you
As a unique human being.
And to be confirmed by you.

We are fully ourselves only in relation to each other;
The I detached from a Thou
Disintegrates.

I do not find you by chance;
I find you by an active life
Of reaching out.

Rather than passively letting things happen to me,
I can act intentionally to make them happen.

I must begin with myself, true;
But I must not end with myself:
The truth begins with two.

†Walter Tubbs, "Beyond Perls," *Journal of Humanistic Psychology*, 12 (Fall 1972), 5.

††Fritz Perls, "Gestalt Prayer." Copyright © Real People Press 1969. All rights reserved. Reprinted with permission.

An experience of this attending love that can be the affirming presence of Christ is witnessed to in a letter a woman wrote to her pastor.

She said that during one of the lowest times in her life she could not imagine what might have happened to her if it had not been for the love and acceptance she received from the people in his church.

She expressed gratitude to God for leading her to the pastor and to these wonderful people.

She said that her journey in the future would probably have its ups and downs but she had hope, because she knew now that forgiveness, acceptance, peace, and health could be hers.

She ended her letter by expressing love to the people in the church.

The indwelling Christ is an affirming presence. As Christs to others we must be affirming presences.

A part of the affirmation of others is *doing good*. When we act in charity toward others, perform deeds of love on their behalf, we reinforce the image of God within them. By sharing our resources with others we become like God, the only one who is good. If that sounds strange, reread the story in Matthew 19:16-26. A wealthy man came to Jesus seeking eternal life. After an exchange that revealed that the fellow was very religious and kept all the commandments, Jesus told him to give his riches to the poor. The conversation that led to that bottom line of giving up his wealth and following Jesus was preceded by Jesus' statement, "Only one is good—God." So the implication is clear—to be like God is to be good by doing good for others, and doing good for others affirms them in their worth.

## Forgiving Presence

Now the second area of crucial concern. As the indwelling Christ is a forgiving presence in our lives, we must be his forgiving presence to others.

The most graphic story of Jesus' ministry of forgiveness is

that of the woman caught in adultery and brought to Jesus for judgment. Those who caught her blazoned her shame before everyone. They also were testing Jesus. If he condemned her, his reputation for understanding and kindness, gentleness and mercy, would be shattered, and no longer would persons be drawn to him and be able to leave with jubilant hearts because of his forgiving love.

What would be better for his detractors would be for Jesus not to condemn her; then this so-called prophet could be completely discredited as one who encouraged adultery.

It took only a look, a call for the *sinless* to cast the first stone, then a word written in the sand, to send the accusers slinking away. And Jesus was left alone with the woman. In a few seconds she learned what she had been seeking all her shameful life—what it really means to love and be loved. It had come in the presence of venomous and stony hearts, when death was only a pile of stones away. The accusers were gone, but the woman was not yet free. Then it came, the transforming word: "Neither do I condemn you; go and sin no more."

In one bold act Jesus had shown her what love is, and kindled that love in her heart. She went away forgiven—*and those who are forgiven much love much!*

Do they? Do we? People around us are dying, shriveling up to a joyless existence, weighed down by guilt to powerlessness, because they lack the freedom, the emotional energy, and spiritual power that forgiveness affords.

There is a troubling word of Jesus recorded in John 20:23: "If you forgive the sins of any, they are forgiven; if you retain the sins of any, they are retained." There are depths of mystery here that we may never plumb, but that gives us no excuse. The onus is upon us, and it should be an exhilarating not a depressing responsibility. We can understand at least this: We are to be the channels of Christ's forgiving grace; and if we aren't, there may be those who will not experience the joyful meaning of that forgiveness.

We can be those channels in a lot of ways, not least of which is *nonjudgmental listening*. Such listening requires a humility on my part, and an honest recognition that I am never immune to "falling," that no matter how *secure* I may be in my present "walk with the Lord" I may slip and stumble, and fall into snares as damaging and destructive as those about which I am hearing from another who has honored me by sharing his or her confession. If I enter a relationship, or listen to a confession more intent on *curing* than *caring* I will not be a channel of Christ's forgiving love. If I care I will listen nonjudgmentally.

We must also *announce* the good news of forgiveness. A primary function of a priest—and all of us as Christians are priests—is to say the word: "In the name of Christ you are forgiven." I have seen it over and over again: persons who have been earnest and sincere in their prayer for forgiveness, and who are themselves forgiving persons, yet cannot get relief for their own guilt; they are not assured of Christ's forgiveness. Then the word is spoken by another Christian, "You are forgiven," and that does it—they know and can accept forgiveness and freedom from guilt. Release and relief comes to others when we are given the grace to hear their confession and take the authority to announce, "In the name of Christ, you are forgiven."

A woman engaged me in conversation following a brief two-hour conference I had given on The Shaping Power of the Indwelling Christ. The sharing that had already taken place in the conference provided a setting of openness that enabled her to move quickly into deep confession. Her father had died two years previously, and for the last year she had been committed to a life of spiritual discipline, involved with a very meaningful prayer group, and had experienced some exceedingly helpful pastoral counseling. In it all she had discovered a deep reservoir of anger toward her father. Tears came to her eyes as she talked about it, her face was strained and her entire body grew tense. The Spirit said to me, "Speak the word." I did—with love and tenderness, but with the strength of solid conviction: "Mary, in the name of Christ, you are forgiven."

Now, it doesn't always happen this way, but it happens often enough so that we know the power and experience the joy of it. Her tears flowed more freely, but now they were tears of joy, her face relaxed and lightened, and her eyes shone through the tears. "Thank you," she said, "Oh, thank you"—the expression of overflowing release and relief. The love and care of her pastor and her prayer group had no doubt prepared her to hear that explicit word. To be channels of such freeing grace is our daily opportunity.

Before we can be transparent channels of the forgiving love of Christ through nonjudgmental listening, by pronouncing the words of forgiveness and in other ways, we must be forgiving persons ourselves. This is evidence of the reality of Christ indwelling us. In this way we are Christ to those we meet.

In our closing chapter we will consider two further aspects of our style of life if we would be Christ to and receive Christ from the people we meet.

# 10

## *Servant Without Portfolio*

"Downward mobilty" is the fresh and vivid metaphor Henry Nouwen has suggested for *life in Christ*. His metaphor is a play on the pervasive image of our technological and intensely competitive society: the uncontrolled drive for *upward mobility*. Almost from the moment we are able to pick up cues the signals are clear: life is a ladder by which we are to climb to the top, or it is a series of battles which we must win in order to gain the reward of success, position, money, power, influence, and prestige. To be a real man or woman is not only to survive the formidable competitive struggle for success, but is to be victorious. Anybody can make it to the top, we are told, if we will just try harder.

In its most blatant expression, upward mobility becomes a perversion of natural and healthy ambition. Making it to the top becomes its own goal, and serving ideas, exploring meaning, and caring for others are lost.

Trina Paulus' book, *Hope for the Flowers*, gives us one of the most graphic and powerful expressions of upward mobility mindless and out of control. She describes her book as "a tale partly about life, partly about revolution, and lots about hope for adults and others (including caterpillars who can read). It is a children's book, in a sense, but for adults; and it is about caterpillars, but more about people."

One day, Stripe, a caterpillar and the main character, was shocked by his own thought that there must be more to life than just eating and getting bigger. So he climbed down from the friendly tree that had shaded and provided him food and he started out *seeking more*. But nothing satisfied him. Other crawlers that he met were so busy eating they had no time to talk, just as Stripe had been, so he concluded they knew no more about life than he.

Then one day he met some crawlers who were really crawling. Their goal was a great column rising high into the air. He joined those driven crawlers and discovered that the column was a pile of squirming, pushing, caterpillars—"a caterpillar pillar." Everybody was struggling to get to the top, but the tip was so lost in the clouds that Stripe nor anyone he questioned had any idea what was there.

Sometimes when I get caught up in the hectic, undirected, often unnamed and unexplained "rat race" which often even characterizes "Christian work," I have dreams (or should I say nightmares?) of Stripe and the contorting, squirming, struggling mass of caterpillars—a column of climbers, pushing and kicking, climbing or being climbed on. One passage from the book gives the picture.

But some days it seemed he could only manage to keep his place. It was especially then that an anxious shadow nagged inside. "What's at the top?" it whispered. "Where are you going?"

On one exasperated day Stripe couldn't stand it any longer and actually yelled back: "I don't know, but there's no time to think about it!"

A little yellow caterpillar he was crawling over gasped: "What did you say?"

"I was just talking to myself," Stripe mumbled. "It really isn't important, I was just wondering where we're going." (*Hope for the Flowers*)

Thoughts like that did not stay with Stripe long. He realized he had lost his singlemindedness. He must move on—to the top!

Now, back to Nouwen. The problem, he says, is not that we have ambition—that is healthy; not the desire for growth and development as an individual or a community, "but in making upward mobility itself a religion." Then he gives us the fresh and vivid image of *downward mobility.* "The story of our salvation stands radically over and against the philosophy of upward mobility. The great paradox which Scripture reveals to us is that real and total freedom can only be found through downward mobility. The Word of God came down to us and lived among us as a slave. The divine way is indeed the downward way."

One of the most beautiful and descriptive words about Jesus is found in Philippians 2:5-11:

Let this mind be in you which was also in Christ Jesus; who, being in the form of God, did not consider equality with God something to be grasped, but emptied Himself by taking the form of a servant, and coming in the likeness of men. And being found in appearance as a man, He humbled Himself and became obedient to the point of death, even the death of the cross. Therefore God also has highly exalted Him and given Him the name which is above every name, that at the name of Jesus every knee should bow, of those in heaven, and of those on earth, and of those under the earth, and that every tongue should confess that Jesus Christ is Lord, to the glory of God the Father. (NKJB-NT)

Not only is this a vivid description of Jesus, it is a call to us. *"Let this mind be in you,* which was also in Christ Jesus; . . . who took the form of a servant." But not many of us want to be servants, do we? Yet, it is clear as we read the New Testament that this was the most distinctive quality of Jesus' style of ministry. And Jesus leaves little doubt that it is the style to which he calls us. "The disciple is not superior to his teacher, nor the slave to his master" (Matt. 10:24 JB). "Anyone who wants to be great among you must be your servant, . . . just as the Son of Man came not to be served but to serve" (Matt. 20:26-28 JB). Not only does Jesus call us to this style, he gives us life through this style: "Anyone who finds his life will lose it; anyone who loses his life for my sake will find it" (Matt. 10:39 JB).

"What is new about this?" you ask. "I have been hearing it all my life." Right. We have been hearing it, but the truth is not yet alive among us. I offer two signals which may put the truth in a fresh light; I hope in such a clear light that the radicalness of it will cause us to consider and wrestle with it anew.

## Servants After the Style of Jesus

The first signal: *there is a vast difference between the way most of us serve and Jesus' call to be a servant.* The way most of us serve keeps us in control. We choose whom, when, where, and how we will serve. We stay in charge. Jesus is calling for something else. He is calling us to be servants. When we make this choice, we give up the right to be in charge. The amazing thing is that when we make this choice we experience great freedom. We become available and vulnerable, and we lose our fear of being stepped on, or manipulated, or taken advantage of. Are not these our basic fears? We do not want to be in a position of weakness.

Jesus' third beatitude addresses our core anxiety. "Blessed are the meek," he said. Meekness means a total dedication to God's plan. The meek person has leaped from the upward mobility ladder and reflects a reversal of attitudes toward possessions, prestige, and power. The meek have taken upon themselves the yoke of Christ. The meek deal with power by serving (Matt. 20:20-28). They handle the problem of possessions by using them on behalf of the poor (Matt. 6:19-34; 19:16-22). The meek deal with rank and prestige by refusing to be put in a box of aloofness and separation from others, and by avoiding any show of titles (Matt. 23:8-12).

The extreme opposite of meekness is violence. More and more ours is becoming a violent society. Violence is the way society deals with power, possession, and prestige. When this seems far removed from me and the "little world" in which I live, I try to own the truth of it by reflecting on how possessive I am, even unconsciously. It doesn't take an extensive inventory of how I live from day to day, the way I spend my time and money, to realize how caught I am in the choking tentacles of my consumer world. The damning thing is that I fall into the subtle but strangling syndrome of protecting my consumer-self, defending my position, my goods, my prestige, my influence and power. Once I heard someone say, "If you and I are alone on an island and you have a loaf of bread and it's the only food we have, you will never sleep." That makes the point clearly. We become possessed by our possessions.

The awful truth is that in our day there is an unbreakable link between, if not a fusion of, consumerism and militarism. This goes beyond individuals and groups and nations; it affects all races and sexes, the rich and the poor. We do well to consider often the word of James:

What causes wars, and what causes fightings among you? Is it not your passions that are at war in your members? You desire and do not have; so you kill. And you covet and cannot obtain; so you fight and wage war. You do not have, because you do not ask. You ask and do not receive, because you ask wrongly, to spend it on your passions. Unfaithful creatures! Do you not know that friendship with the world is enmity with God? Therefore whoever wishes to be a friend of the world makes himself an enemy to God. Or do you suppose it is in vain that the scripture says, "He yearns jealously over the spirit which he has made to dwell in us"? But he gives more grace; therefore it says, "God opposes the proud, but gives grace to the humble." Submit yourselves therefore to God. Resist the devil and he will flee from you. Draw near to God and he will draw near to you. Cleanse your hands, you sinners, and purify your hearts, you men of double mind. Be wretched and mourn and weep. Let your laughter be turned to mourning and your joy to dejection. Humble yourselves before the Lord and he will exalt you. (James 4:1-10)

It is a scathing and stunning word but it supports Jesus' beatitude, "Blessed are the meek." Possessions, position, and power, not approached with meekness, generate mistrust, severing of relationships, even violence. Meekness generates reconciliation and caring. It is the telling mark of a servant after the style of Jesus.

Return to my earlier assertion that when we become servants after the style of Jesus, when we give up the right to be in control and to choose, we experience freedom. Jesus said that the meek inherit the earth and servants become masters. As servants, we *have* the earth, we are masters because we are free; we are no longer controlled by possessions, power, or prestige. When we make the deliberate choice to be servants, we have made the decision that has ultimate meaning and shapes our whole life. Strength, vitality, joy, and meaning are ours when we act out of being a servant, rather than the pride-producing choices of serving now and then as we please.

## *The Downward Way—God's Way*

That leads to the second signal which I hope will bring feeling back into our anesthetized wills so that we may be servants in the style of Jesus. I use "feeling" and "will" together, though we usually separate emotion from volition. Being a servant is neither a matter of our own feeling nor our own will, yet incorporates both. The old hymn is right: "My will is not my own 'till I have made it thine." Again Henri Nouwen warns us rightly:

When we think that living the downward way is within our reach and that our task is simply to imitate Christ, we have misunderstood the basic truth which has been revealed to us.

The downward way is God's way, not ours. God reveals himself as God to us in the downward pull, because only he who is God can empty himself of his divine privileges and become as we are. . . .

The spiritual life . . . is the life in which the Spirit of Christ, who reaches the depths of God, is given to us so that we may know, with a new knowledge of mind and heart, the way of God. (*Sojourners*, June 1981)

This is what I was saying in chapter 8. There is a difference between *following* Christ and being *in Christ*. Alive *in Christ*, we become those who are "little Christs" as Luther said, living in all places and all times. Shaped by the indwelling Christ, we receive new eyes to see, new ears to hear, and new hands to touch.

The downward mobility of God, becomes our way not because we try to imitate Jesus, but because we are transformed into living Christs by his Spirit. The spiritual life is the life of the Spirit of Christ in us, a life that sets us free to be strong while weak, to be free while captive, to be joyful while in pain, to be rich while poor, to be on the downward way of salvation while living in the midst of an upwardly mobile society. (*Sojourners*, June 1981)

I titled this chapter "servants without portfolio" to make the point that being Christ to and/or receiving Christ from every person we meet is the characteristic expression of the indwelling Christ. Ambassadors in governmental service of the United States are usually assigned to particular geographical locales; they have a *portfolio*. It may be Russia, Great Britain, Mexico. Occasionally there are persons designated ambassadors "at large" or "without portfolio." They do not have any one particular assignment but are sent wherever there is need for their services. As persons in Christ, we are "servants without portfolio." Everywhere, at all times, we are servants. This is the mind of Christ in fullness within us, expressed in all of life.

## Compassion

To further underscore this fact, I want to talk about the characteristic element of this Christ-style. That element is *compassion*.

The fourteenth-century mystic Walter Hilton based the spiritual life on the twin virtues of meekness and charity. I believe those virtues express themselves in *compassion*. When we are meek and when we love, compassion flows from us to others.

I did not learn the Hebrew language in theology school, but my Old Testament professor, Dr. Boone Bowen, introduced me to the richness of that language. His favorite word—which he contended was descriptive of God and was to characterize all of God's people—was *hesed*. My memory rings with the deep, bass resonance of Dr. Bowen's sounding of that Hebrew word. But more, my mind is filled with the right meaning of it as he interpreted it for his students. *Hesed* is sometimes translated as "compassion," sometimes as "mercy," sometimes as "pity." Dr. Bowen kept reminding us of the inadequacy of one-word translations of *hesed* in English, Greek, or in Latin. What is missing in every one-word translation is the dimension of action that the Hebrew language implies. The Hebrew talks of "doing *hesed* with someone." The word is often connected with *mispat*, the Hebrew word we translate "right" or "justice." So Micah 6:8 reads, "What does Yahweh ask of you except to do *hesed* (compassion) and to love *mispat* (justice)." Today's English Version of that verse is a good one. What God requires of us is this: "to do what is just, to show constant love, and to live in humble fellowship with our God."

*Hesed* is more than a sentiment of love and pity. It demands a "volitional attitude." That is what distinguishes biblical love from current usage of the word. Biblical love includes justice and even judgment. That is the reason I began this discussion of compassion by identifying it as an outward expression of the twin virtues of Christian spirituality: *meekness and love*.

I want now to identify two explicit aspects of compassion which have special relevance to our being "little Christs" to others.

The first is, as Matthew Fox has so well said, that "compassion is not knowing about the suffering and pain of others. It is, in some way, knowing that pain, entering into it, sharing it and tasting it in so far as possible." (I heartily recommend Fox's helpful book *A Spirituality Named Compassion* [Winston Press, 1971].) We are not simply called to know that others suffer, or to assess the painful situations in which they may be, we are to feel the other's feelings. And not only feel the other's feeling, but act on behalf of the other.

This is at least a part of what it means to be *in solidarity with* the poor and oppressed of the world. But that is so difficult, even for those who feel deeply the call to be so identified. I am working on that in my own life and am constantly driven to confession of and deep penitence for my failure. There are three ports of entry in experiencing solidarity which are proving meaningful to me. The first is *direct action*. Where possible, I must act. The epistle of James says it clearly.

If a brother or sister is ill-clad and in lack of daily food, and one of you says to them, "Go in peace, be warmed and filled," without giving them the things needed for the body, what does it profit?
You see that a man is justified by works and not by faith alone.
For as the body apart from the spirit is dead, so faith apart from works is dead. (James 2:15-16, 24, 26)

The second port of entry into solidarity with the poor and oppressed is the *stewardship* of my money and other resources. I control the way I spend my money and I make the decision as to how I will use the resources that are mine. Meekness and love expressed as compassion extend to every area of social and political concern. The resources of the land itself and my use of the natural resources God provides is a matter of concern. The compassionate hear the ancient word of the Lord, knowing that judgment is in the words because of the way we have wasted and polluted and exploited: "Do not defile the land in which you live and in the midst of which I dwell" (Num. 35:34).

The third expression of solidarity with the poor and oppressed is through prayer, especially intercession—seeking to identify with and reach out to the hurting of the world. Apart from being subversive and giving us a vision (as we discussed in chapter 8) in a mysterious way that we can never understand, through prayer, especially intercession, we not only identify with, but take upon ourselves the suffering of others. So, rather than being privatistic, intercession is intensely social. Douglas V. Steere has made the point that in Christian intercession we enter into a great sweep of intercession (solidarity) that is already going on.

For the agony of Christ that shall last until the end of the world is precisely this intercession for the souls of men and women in the world. This state of loving siege at the inner window never ceases, and when I pray for another, I join with God and Christ and the communion of dedicated souls in something that is already operative. Yet this eternal pleading or redemptive process, if we dare speak of so great a mystery, seems to be aided by—yes, even to require—my prayer, my sacrificial readiness to carry another, and to face the cost of this carrying as the final surge that may liberate his soul. *(Dimensions of Prayer)*

Prayer then, especially intercession, is an expression of our greatest love and is a gateway to solidarity. Instead of keeping pain away from us, loving prayer leads us into the suffering of God and of others. The deeper our love of God, the more we will suffer. The more we suffer, the more we will pray.

Our suffering and the suffering of others is embraced by the compassionate Christ, in a way that we may never fully understand; our intercession, through identity with suffering, becomes a channel of Christ's liberating power.

The prime enemy of compassion is injustice. That leads to the second aspect of compassion that has special relevance to our being "little Christs" to others. Just as intercession is never privatistic, so the whole of our compassion must not be. Compassion is social, leading to justice-making action in the public and political areas of life.

There is a sense in which the definition of sin most appropriate for our day in this: "sin is a flight from compassion." Jim Wallis has described the result of such a flight from compassion in one area of our nation's life.

The maximum amount of money ever spent in one year for the entire poverty program equalled the cost of three weeks of the Vietnam War. While it has become politically chic to criticize the failure of government spending to solve social problems, the true blame for the death of public resources for the poor must be placed with the Vietnam War and, more recently, with the escalating military budget. In the meantime, through tax subsidies and other transfer payments, the use of public money to support major corporations and the affluent has far exceeded all government assistance to the poor. This is the biggest scandal of "the welfare state"—a system that allocates most of its resources to make war and subsidize the rich, leaving the poor with precious little except the bum rap of being called "welfare cheaters." When the government tightens its belt, it tightens it around the necks of the poor. Services are cut in the ghettoes, and restrictions are added that further dehumanize welfare recipients, most of whom would prefer the dignity of jobs. (*The Call to Conversion*)

Alive in Christ, we are called to be instruments of blessing for those Jesus said would be blessed. His Beatitudes form the charter for the kingdom in which we live, living in him. These beatitudes outline the core values that are to be incorporated in our lives, and for which we must contend on behalf of others. The poor in spirit and in substance are blessed; they know their need of God. Comfort is promised to those who have learned to cry for the world. The meek are the ones to whom the earth belongs and they will eventually possess it. Those who are hungry for justice and who show mercy will find meaning and will receive mercy. The pure in heart, not the manipulators and controllers, will see God. The peacemakers—they will be blessed and will be called God's own children. To climax it all, because he knows it will happen, Jesus blesses those who suffer unjustly for the cause of compassionate justice. To them he promised the kingdom.

To be Christ to others is to be instruments of blessing for those Jesus said would be blessed, and this calls often for political action and social witness that expresses outrage against systems and institutions that take no account of the needs of the poor and oppressed.

Aristides described the Christians to the Roman emperor Hadrian in a way that gives us pause to consider how well we are acting out our call to be servants without portfolio.

They love one another. They never fail to help widows; they save orphans from those who would hurt them. If they have something they give freely to the man who has nothing; if they see a stranger, they take him home, and are happy, as though he were a real brother. They don't consider themselves brothers in the usual sense, but brothers instead through the Spirit, in God. (*Apology* 15, in *The Anti-Nicene Fathers*, ed. Allan Menzies, 5th edition, New York: Charles Scribner's Sons, 1926)

As Christ comes alive in us, it will be said of us as it was said of the God whom Christ reveals: "The Lord's unfailing love and mercy [compassion] still continue, fresh as the morning, as sure as the sunrise" (Lam. 3:22-23 TEV).

So now we must conclude, but how? In talking about his longing for Christ to come alive in his friends in Galatia, Paul used the image of giving birth to a child. "Oh, my dear children, I feel the pangs of childbirth all over again till Christ be formed within you" (Gal. 4:19 Phillips). Rachel Richardson Smith reflected on the meaning of the Incarnation in light of her own pregnancy and giving birth. She said,

In pregnancy a woman's body takes over. . . . I felt as though I had lost control of my body. It went ahead on its own and left me in shock somewhere behind. . . . In pregnancy I became one with my body as at no other time in my life.

She went on to speak of a woman's being intricately bound up with the new person within her, even though distinct from it. "The two are one," she says,

> and herein lies the paradox. The pregnant woman is both herself and this other being. The two are distinct from each other, though they are not separate.
>
> This too is the paradox of incarnation. . . . God is both Christ and other than Christ. Though not separate from Christ, God is distinct from Christ. . . . Christ is not all of God, as the newborn baby is not all of the mother. But in Christ, God gives birth to God. (*The Christian Century*, Dec. 19, 1979)

We may extend the use of that image for our life in Christ, for in us the Incarnation continues. I am not all of Christ, even as the newborn baby is not all of the mother, and even as Jesus Christ is not all of God. But by an incomprehensible work of grace, Christ is alive in me, and to the degree of my yieldedness to his indwelling presence, I live Christ's life, and I can be Christ to others.

Someone said of Mother Teresa of Calcutta, "She gave herself to Christ and through him to her neighbor. This was the end of her biography and the beginning of her life." Mother Teresa is a transparent witness to the shaping power of the indwelling Christ, a servant without portfolio. So I am going to continue my ritual in one form or another. Maybe, by my response to that glorious possibility, the grace of God will work such a miracle in me, and I will give my life so completely to Christ, and through him to my neighbor, that my biography will end and my life begin. I close then as I began, and invite you to affirm for yourself as I keep affirming for myself: "Maxie, the secret is simply this: Christ *in you*! Yes, Christ *in you*, bringing with him the hope of all the glorious things to come."

## Acknowledgments

*This page is hereby made a part of the copyright page.*

Quotations on pages 23, 49, 111, and 113 are from *A Man in Christ* by James Stewart. Reprinted by permission of Hodder & Stoughton Limited.

The quotation on page 32 is reprinted courtesy *PSA* magazine carried aboard Pacific Southwest Airlines. © 1980. East/West Networks, Inc. publisher.

The quotation by John Cobb on pages 85-86 is from *Haelan*, Diane Vale, editor, © 1981 Institute for Advanced Pastoral Studies, Southfield, Mi., No 2, Spring 1981. Used by permission of John Cobb and the Institute for Advanced Pastoral Studies.

Henri Nouwen's quotations on page 135 and 152-53 are from the article "The Selfless Way of Christ," *Sojourners,* June 1981. Used by permission of the author.

The quotation on pages 137-38 is from *Letters from the Desert* by Carlo Carretto. © 1972 by Orbis Books and Darton, Longman & Todd, Ltd., publishers. Used by permission.

The excerpts on pages 158-59 are from the article "Pregnancy and Childbirth: A Theological Event" by Rachel Richardson Smith. Copyright 1979 Christian Century Foundation. Reprinted by permission from the December 19, 1979 issue of *The Christian Century.*